Praise for *The IBM Data Governance Unified Process*

Data Governance is vital to the success of Master Data Management (MDM) projects—both initially and on an ongoing basis. During 2010 and 2011, Global 5000-size enterprises will increasingly mandate that "no MDM program be funded without the prerequisite Data Governance framework."

"Go Governance, Go Early" is the rallying cry of savvy enterprise and solution architects, who are chartered with setting the scope and direction of their enterprise's data integration programs. Understanding the scope, diversity, and integration challenges is tremendously challenging. Nonetheless, business and IT leadership chartered with defining and executing MDM programs needs help to understand and navigate the numerous Data Governance options. Solutions architects, directors of Data Governance, MDM program managers— all are encouraged to get a fast track to "Go Governance, Go Early" by reading and applying these excellent best practices, accelerators, and models gleaned by Sunil Soares in this much-needed introduction to enterprise-strength Data Governance.

Aaron Zornes
Chief Research Officer, The MDM Institute
Conference Chairman, The "MDM and Data Governance Summit"
Global Conferences Series

Air Products is 18 months into implementing a major Data Governance program. It is a difficult, but very exciting and fulfilling, journey. There are a large number of steps involved in order to make it a success, most of which are new and unfamiliar. There is plenty of advice out there from data management groups and vendors; however, there are many ways of tackling each problem, and the program must be tailored to each company's needs and situation. The IBM Data Governance Unified Process, as detailed by Sunil Soares, is an order of magnitude more comprehensive than anything we have seen to date. It is very clear that the author has been informed by a vast amount of practical experience across many types of companies and brings a refreshing, down-to-earth approach to this discipline. Although one purpose of the book is to recommend technology approaches, its great merit is that it recognizes that the core issues to be tackled first are fundamentally not about technology but about people and process. The book lays out these issues in a vendor-neutral way.

Tony Harris
Enterprise Data Architect
Air Products

Data Governance is a critical process but is rarely recognized as such until the crisis arrives—reports don't cross-foot; executives disagree on the status of key measures; security breaches and compliance exposures surface to the worst people at the worst moments; and the costs of multiple, conflicting copies of information spiral out of control. Wouldn't it be wonderful if we could believe that organizations can tackle the problems Data Governance can prevent, before the dashboards all go red?

Sunil Soares believes they can. In this excellent discussion, he walks the reader through the strategy, the process, and the tools of the trade to do so. Naturally, the examples are IBM tools, and that's not an accident. But this is not a sales pitch; it's a guide to successfully solving a potentially devastating problem. Read it, and reap.

Merv Adrian
IT Market Strategy

The business world is a dynamic and challenging landscape. Business leaders are constantly challenged to adapt and apply their expertise and experience to fluctuating market conditions, in order to sustain business success. The turn of the millennium has seen the onset of the Information Age, marked by the strategic role of information and data in driving business operations, enabling strategic decision-making, and empowering organizations to leverage data to achieve a competitive edge in the market. Individuals, communities, businesses, governments, and social organizations are most certainly influenced and impacted by the Information Age. Most business success stories hinge on the creative and strategic leveraging of data living in the enterprise. In the Information Age, data is a strategic corporate asset, and must be managed as such.

The principles of Data Governance outline how to achieve that management discipline, ensuring that organizations continue to enjoy the benefits of their data. Sunil Soares, a key member of the IBM team, has detailed the ABCs of Data Governance in this book. He has expertly packaged the content, which comprises theory supported by relevant examples gleaned from his engagements with numerous business partners around the globe.

This work is a practical manual for business leaders to adopt in their Data Governance implementations. As the saying goes,"Why reinvent the wheel when somebody else has perfected the model?" The IBM team has defined the model for Data Governance. It is available, through this book, for business leaders to embrace and adopt, in order to ensure success with their implementations.

I have had the pleasure of engaging directly with the author on the Data Governance project in my organization. Sunil is an expert in his field; he lives the subject, has a wealth of knowledge on the subject, and is passionate about Data Governance. He goes about coaching and advising organizations in a professional yet simple manner that endears him to his clients. The time that I spent under Sunil's wing was invaluable to me and my organization. The author's endearing qualities shine in this book, which makes for absorbing reading. I am certain that you too will enjoy and appreciate this book for the many invaluable insights contained in it. Thank you, Sunil, for empowering us Data Governance practitioners with your expertise.

If you are part of a Data Governance project, I wish you great success in your endeavors.

Komalin Chetty
Data Governance Champion,
Telkom South Africa

The IBM Data Governance Unified Process
Driving Business Value with IBM Software and Best Practices

Sunil Soares

MC Press Online, LLC
Ketchum, ID 83340

The IBM Data Governance Unified Process
Sunil Soares

First Edition
First Printing—September 2010

MC Press offers excellent discounts on this book when ordered in quantity for bulk purchases or special sales, which may include custom covers and content particular to your business, training goals, marketing focus, and branding interest.

MC Press Online, LLC
    Corporate Offices
    P.O. Box 4886
    Ketchum, ID 83340-4886 USA
For information regarding sales and/or customer service, please contact:
    MC Press
    P.O. Box 4300
    Big Sandy, TX 75755-4300 USA
For information regarding permissions or special orders, please contact:
    mcbooks@mcpressonline.com

ISBN: 978-158347-360-3

I would like to convey my special thanks and appreciation to Maya Soares, Lizzie Soares, Helena Soares, Cecilia Soares, and Hubert Soares for their great support during the development of this book.

Acknowledgments

Ensuring the appropriate treatment for a complex topic such as Data Governance required participation from a number of thought leaders both inside and outside IBM. The creation of this book was a team effort, and I want to thank a number of individuals.

I want to thank Arvind Krishna, Bob Keseley, Dave Laverty, Inhi Cho, Paraic Sweeney, Piyush Gupta, Tom Inman, and Mike Nolan for their sponsorship of Data Governance as a critical initiative at IBM.

I especially want to thank Steve Adler who, through his strong leadership at the helm of the IBM Data Governance Council for the past five years, has been instrumental in coalescing Data Governance into a unique discipline with an emerging community of practitioners.

I want to thank a number of individuals for their contributions to this book:

- Ken Bisconti, Craig Rhinehart, Laurence Leong, and Paula Fricker for their market-leading activities in the area of Information Lifecycle Governance

- David Corrigan and Ian Stahl for their insights on Master Data Governance

- Michael Dziekan for his extensive experience with Business Intelligence Competency Centers

- Farnaz Erfan, Beate Porst, and Steven Totman for their excellent work on business glossaries and metadata

- Todd Goldman and Alex Gorelik for their content on data discovery

- Brett Gow for his practitioner-level insights on Data Governance

- Bill Mathews for his experience in advising IBM Insurance clients and sharing Data Governance best practices

- Marty Moseley for his overall perspectives on Master Data Governance, as well as his work on Data Governance declarations in Appendix E of this book

- Eric Naiburg for his input on all topics related to IBM Software

- Phil Neray and Brian Roosevelt for their excellent insight into topics related to data security and compliance

- Arvind Sathi for his experience in Data Governance topics within the telecommunications industry

- Helena Soares for her terrific edits to the manuscript

- Wayne Wilczynski for his experience in advising IBM banking and financial markets clients and sharing the best practices used in the real world

Also, I want to thank Michael Curry, Glenn Hintze, Jan Shauer, Steven Stansel, and Susan Visser from IBM, Tony Harris from Air Products, Sebastian Gass from Chevron, and Michael O'Connor from KeyCorp for their advice and insight during the authorship of this book.

Table of Contents

Foreword by Arvind Krishna

IBM has been at the forefront of the Information Governance movement since the formation of the IBM Data Governance Council in 2005. We've worked closely with industry-leading companies from around the world to tackle the biggest challenges associated with governance. Information Governance had its roots in compliance and risk, but over the past few years we've been observing a shift to leverage it for value creation as much as risk mitigation.

There are different levels of maturity to an organization's Information Governance approach and adoption of technology. What might be optimal for one enterprise is not for another. The organizational structure, roles, and foundational capabilities are a key part of the equation for success.

Every company has multiple information supply chains that can be optimized. The challenge most organizations face today is that they can't identify their information supply chains, much less manage them to exploit new business insights consistently and pervasively across the organization.

IBM has assembled a comprehensive approach to Information Governance that delivers the industry's strongest portfolio of products, services, and best practices to address every organization's needs. This book provides a practical set of detailed steps and sub-steps to implement an Information Governance program, as well as the associated automation provided by IBM Software.

Arvind Krishna
General Manager,
Information Management
IBM

Foreword by Michael Schroeck

Today, organizations around the world understand the importance and value of their information assets. At the same time, executives are not fully leveraging this information, due to the lack of accuracy, consistency, relevance, and timeliness. As a result, Information Governance has moved to the forefront, as companies struggle with how to effectively design and implement an Information Governance program. This book provides the answer by describing a proven, comprehensive, and practical approach to enterprise Information Governance. It is a must-read for both experienced Information Governance professionals as well as those who are new to this area.

Only through the application of the principles described in the following pages will organizations truly be able to maximize the value of their information, which is necessary to become a "smarter" company.

Michael Schroeck
Partner and Global Leader,
BAO Analytics Solutions Team and Center of Competence,
IBM Global Services

Introduction by Steve Adler

Recently, I applied for a car loan from my bank. The online application process was fantastic and saved so much time that otherwise would have been spent in a branch office or on the phone. I got an acceptance quote and interest rate within 60 seconds. Minutes later, I called the bank to complete the process. Unfortunately, I made a mistake when I classified the loan as a refinance—it was actually a lease buyout. I couldn't change the form online once it was submitted, and the call center representatives couldn't do it either. So, I had to cancel that application and do it again. Again, it took just a couple of minutes to fill out the form and get a quote back, and, once again, I was on the phone talking to the representative.

A few days later, I went into the branch to complete the transaction. The branch manager was charming and helpful and, after signing about 30 different forms, I walked out with my car refinanced. Three days later, the leasing company called to say that two forms were missing from the application that had been forwarded by the bank. I called the bank, but the representatives there were clueless. "The leasing company must be wrong," they said. I called the leasing company, and back and forth it went, until I agreed to go back to the bank and re-sign the forms. Then I started getting email messages from the bank, informing me that my original online quote was still approved and pending my action— even though I was sure the bank told me it had cancelled that quote.

This kind of normal, everyday Data Governance problem besets every business. I've seen a lot worse. Most people just call them mistakes, but they can lead to lost business, increased risk, and certainly extra cost. Whether you have a formal Data Governance program or not, your organization has Data Governance problems like these, and many others as well. You know it, and your customers know it.

Once you recognize this problem, the choice is pretty simple: you can either deal with it or ignore it. Since you are reading this book, you've decided not to ignore it. Good.

Your next decision is how to deal with it. Mistakes are a part of life. Your business makes them because people run your business. The data didn't get wrong on its own. You need to change the way the people who run your business think about data, what they do with it, and how they build businesses that use data in the first place. To do that, you need a system, a Data Governance program that helps bring people together, to coordinate, collaborate, and communicate.

This book has some important tools to get you started the right way toward building a Data Governance program, which can fix the simple, and complex, errors and omissions your organization makes every day.

You already made the most important decision, in buying this book. Now finish the book and start your program, because time is not on your side. In the few minutes it took you to read this, someone somewhere in your organization has dropped a few forms, miscoded a new account, or sent duplicate bills to a customer.

The clock is ticking. . . .

Steve Adler
Chairman,
IBM Data Governance Council

1

Introduction to Data Governance

Data Governance is the discipline of treating data as an enterprise asset. It involves the exercise of decision rights to optimize, secure, and leverage data as an enterprise asset. It involves the orchestration of people, process, technology, and policy within an organization, to derive the optimal value from enterprise data. Data Governance plays a pivotal role in aligning the disparate, stovepiped, and often conflicting policies that cause data anomalies in the first place.

Much like in the early days of Customer Relationship Management (CRM), organizations are starting to appoint full-time or part-time owners of Data Governance. As with any emerging discipline, there are multiple definitions of Data Governance, but the market is starting to crystallize around the definition of treating data as an asset.

Traditional accounting rules do not allow companies to treat data as a financial asset on their balance sheets, unless it has been purchased from an external entity. Despite this conservative accounting treatment, enterprises now understand that their data should be treated as an asset similar to plant and equipment.

Treating data as a strategic enterprise asset implies that organizations need to build inventories of their existing data, just as they would for physical assets. The typical organization has an excessive amount of data about its customers, vendors, and products. The organization might not even know where all this data is located. This can pose challenges, especially in the case of *personally identifiable information* (*PII*). Organizations need to secure business-critical data within their financial, Enterprise Resource Planning, and human resource applications from unauthorized changes, since this can affect the integrity of their financial reporting, as well as the quality and reliability of daily business decisions. They must also protect sensitive customer information such as credit card numbers and PII data, as well as intellectual property such as customer lists, product designs, and proprietary algorithms from both internal and external threats. Finally, organizations need to get the maximum value out of their data, driving initiatives such as improved risk management and customer-centricity.

Data is at once an organization's greatest source of value and its greatest source of risk. Poor data management often means poor business decisions and greater exposure to compliance violations and theft. For example, regulations such as Sarbanes-Oxley in the United States, the equivalent European Sarbanes-Oxley, and the Japanese Financial Instruments and Exchange Law (J-SOX) dictate a balance between restricted access and the appropriate use of data, as mandated by rules, policies, and regulations. On the other hand, the ability to leverage clean, trusted data can help organizations provide better service, drive customer loyalty, spend less effort complying with regulations and reporting, and increase innovation.

Organizations must also consider the business value of their unstructured data. This unstructured data, often referred to as *content*, needs to be governed just as structured data does.

A good example of unstructured data governance is setting records management policy. Many companies are required to maintain electronic and paper records for a given period of time. They need to produce these records quickly and cost-effectively during the legal discovery process. They also need to be in compliance with the established retention schedules for specific document types. Several organizations use the term "Information Governance" to define this program. Although we use the terms "data" and "information" interchangeably, we will stick with the more commonly used term "Data Governance" throughout this book.

Here are some benefits that organizations can derive by governing their data:

- Improve the level of trust that users have in reports
- Ensure consistency of data across multiple reports from different parts of the organization

- Ensure appropriate safeguards over corporate information to satisfy the demands of auditors and regulators

- Improve the level of customer insight to drive marketing initiatives

- Directly impact the three factors an organization most cares about: increasing revenue, lowering costs, and reducing risk

Founded in November 2004 by Steve Adler, the IBM® Data Governance Council is a leadership forum for practitioners such as Data Governance leaders, Information Governance leaders, chief data officers, enterprise data architects, chief information security officers, chief risk officers, chief compliance officers, and chief privacy officers. The council is concerned with issues related to how an organization can effectively govern data as an enterprise asset. It focuses on the relationships among information, business processes, and the value of information to the organization.

According to findings published by Adler for the IBM Data Governance Council in the whitepaper *The IBM Data Governance Maturity Model: Building a Roadmap for Effective Data Governance*, these are the top Data Governance challenges today:

- Inconsistent Data Governance can cause a disconnect between business goals and IT programs.

- Governance policies are not linked to structured requirements-gathering and reporting.

- Risks are not addressed from a lifecycle perspective with common data repositories, policies, standards, and calculation processes.

- Metadata and business glossaries are not used to bridge semantic differences across multiple applications in global enterprises.

- Few technologies exist today to assess data asset values that link security, privacy, and compliance.

- Controls and architectures are deployed before long-term consequences are modeled.

- Governance across different data domains and organizational boundaries can be difficult to implement.

- What exactly needs to be governed is often unclear.

- Data Governance has strategic and tactical elements, which are not always clearly defined.

Data Governance is about decision rights and influencing human behavior. This book is a practitioner's guide based on real-life experiences with organizations that have implemented similar programs. It highlights specific areas where IBM software tools and best practices support the process of Data Governance.

2

The IBM Data Governance Unified Process

The benefits of a commitment to a comprehensive enterprise Data Governance initiative are many and varied, and so are the challenges to achieving strong Data Governance.

Many enterprises have requested a process manual that lays out the steps to implement a Data Governance program. Obviously, every enterprise will implement Data Governance differently, mainly due to differing business objectives. Some enterprises might focus on data quality, others on customer-centricity, and still others on ensuring the privacy of sensitive customer data. Some organizations will embrace a formal Data Governance program, while others will want to implement something that is more lightweight and tactical.

Regardless of these details, every organization should perform certain steps to govern its data. The IBM Data Governance Unified Process shown in Figure 2.1 maps out these 14 major steps (ten required steps and four optional tracks), along with the associated IBM software tools and best practices to support an effective Data Governance program.

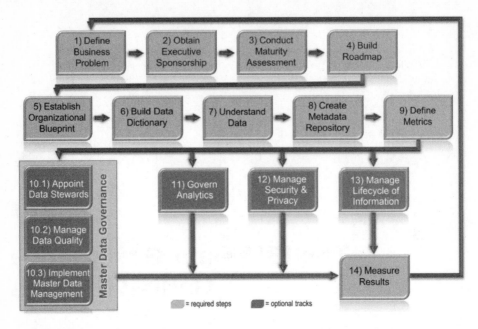

Figure 2.1: An overview of the IBM Data Governance Unified Process.

The ten required steps are necessary to lay the foundations for an effective Data Governance program. An enterprise will then select one or more of the four optional tracks, namely Master Data Governance, Analytics Governance, Security and Privacy, and Information Lifecycle Governance. Finally, the Data Governance Unified Process needs to be measured, and the results conveyed to executive sponsors, on a regular basis.

Let's walk through the steps in the figure in further detail:

1. Define the business problem.

The main reason that Data Governance programs fail is that they do not identify a tangible business problem. It is imperative that the organization defines the initial scope of the Data Governance program around a specific business problem, such as a failed audit, a data breach, or the need for improved data quality for risk-management purposes. Once the Data Governance program begins to tackle the identified business problems, it will receive support from the business functions to extend its scope to additional areas.

2. *Obtain executive sponsorship.*

It is important to establish sponsorship from key IT and business executives for the Data Governance program. The best way to obtain this sponsorship is to establish value in terms of a business case and "quick hits." For example, the business case might be focused on householding and name-matching, to improve the quality of data to support a customer-centricity program.

As with any important program, the organization needs to appoint an overall owner of Data Governance. Organizations have historically identified the chief information security officer as the owner of Data Governance. Today, however, the ownership of Data Governance tends to reside within the CIO's office, in either the business intelligence or data architecture area. Data Governance leadership might also reside with the chief risk officer, especially in banks. A growing number of enterprises are staffing Data Governance roles on a full-time basis, with titles such as "data steward" indicating the importance of treating data as an enterprise asset. Regardless of title, the responsibility assigned to this role must be high enough in the executive ranks to ensure that the Data Governance program drives meaningful change.

3. *Conduct a maturity assessment.*

Every organization needs to conduct an assessment of its Data Governance maturity, preferably on an annual basis. The IBM Data Governance Council has developed a maturity model based on 11 categories (discussed in Chapter 5), such as "Data Risk Management and Compliance," " Value Creation," and "Stewardship." The Data Governance organization needs to assess the organization's current level of maturity (current state) and the desired future level of maturity (future state), which is typically 12 to 18 months out. This duration must be long enough to produce results, yet short enough to ensure continued buy-in from key stakeholders.

4. *Build a roadmap.*

The Data Governance organization needs to develop a roadmap to bridge the gap between the current state and the desired future state for the 11 categories of Data Governance maturity. For example, the Data Governance organization might review the maturity gap for Stewardship and determine that the enterprise needs to appoint data stewards to focus on targeted subject areas such as customer, vendor, and product. The Data Governance program also needs to include "quick hits"—areas where the initiative can drive near-term business value.

5. *Establish an organizational blueprint.*

The Data Governance organization needs to build a charter to govern its operations, and to ensure that it has enough authority to act as a tiebreaker in critical situations. Data Governance organizations operate best in a three-tier format. The top tier is the Data Governance council, which consists of the key functional and business leaders who rely on data as an enterprise asset. The middle tier is the Data Governance working group, which consists of middle managers who meet more frequently. The final tier consists of the data stewardship community, which is responsible for the quality of the data on a day-to-day basis.

6. *Build the data dictionary.*

Effective management of business terms can help ensure that the same descriptive language applies throughout the organization. A data dictionary or business glossary is a repository with definitions of key terms. It is used to gain consistency and agreement between the technical and business sides of an organization. For example, what is the definition of a "customer"? Is a customer someone who has made a purchase, or someone who is considering a purchase? Is a former employee still categorized as an "employee"? Are the terms "partner" and "reseller" synonymous? These questions can be answered by building a common data dictionary. Once implemented, the data dictionary can span the organization to ensure that business terms are tied via metadata to technical terms, and that the organization has a single, common understanding.

7. *Understand the data.*

Someone once said, "You cannot govern what you do not first understand." Few applications stand alone today. Rather, they are made up of systems, and "systems of systems," with applications and databases strewn all over the enterprise, yet integrated, or at least interrelated. The relational database model actually makes matters worse by fragmenting business entities for storage. But how is everything related? The Data Governance team needs to discover the critical data relationships across the enterprise.

Data discovery may include simple and hard-to-find relationships, as well as the locations of sensitive data within the enterprise's IT systems.

8. *Create a metadata repository.*

Metadata is data about data. It is information regarding the characteristics of any data artifact, such as its technical name, business name, location, perceived importance, and relationships to other data artifacts in the enterprise. The Data Governance program will generate a lot of business metadata from the data dictionary and a lot of technical metadata during the discovery phase. This metadata needs to be stored in a repository so that it can be shared and leveraged across multiple projects.

9. *Define metrics.*

Data Governance needs to have robust metrics to measure and track progress. The Data Governance team must recognize that when you measure something, performance improves. As a result, the Data Governance team must pick a few Key Performance Indicators (KPIs) to measure the ongoing performance of the program. For example, a bank will want to assess the overall credit exposure by industry. In that case, the Data Governance program might select the percentage of null Standard Industry Classification (SIC) codes as a KPI, to track the quality of risk management information.

These are the first nine required steps. The final required step is discussed later in this chapter. The enterprise also needs to select at least one of the four optional Data Governance tracks (Master Data Governance, Analytics Governance, Security and Privacy, and Information Lifecycle Governance).

Let's select the Master Data Governance optional track and walk through the application of its required sub-steps. The organization will need to ensure that the business problem (such as customer-centricity) is clearly articulated, and that executive sponsors are identified in the business and in IT. The organization will conduct a short Data Governance maturity assessment and define a roadmap. There needs to be some level of Data Governance organization to align the business and IT, to ensure near-term benefits. Business terms such as "customer" need to be clearly defined, especially if "customer" is one of the master data domains. The Data Governance organization needs to understand existing data sources and critical data elements. The business definitions, and the technical metadata from the discovery process, need to be captured within a metadata repository. Finally, the Data Governance organization needs to establish KPIs, such as a reduction in customer duplicates, to measure the ongoing performance of the Master Data Governance program.

The level of emphasis on the required steps will vary based on the optional tracks that have been selected for Data Governance. As an example, let's review how step 7 ("Understand the Data") might be applied differently, based on the optional track or tracks selected. The Master Data Governance track will involve understanding the critical data elements to facilitate the mapping of sources to targets. The Analytics Governance track will involve understanding the relationship between key reports and critical data elements. The Security and Privacy track will involve understanding the location of sensitive data. Finally, the Information Lifecycle Governance track will enable the enterprise to understand the location of business objects, such as customer, as a precursor to an archiving project.

We will discuss these topics in greater detail in subsequent chapters, so we will just cover a few sample questions and potential focus areas for the remainder of this chapter. Here is a short description of the optional tracks within the IBM Data Governance Unified Process:

10. *Govern master data.*

> The most valuable information within an enterprise—the business-critical data about customers, products, materials, vendors, and accounts—is commonly known as *master data*. Despite its importance, master data is often replicated and scattered across business processes, systems, and applications throughout the enterprise. Governing master data is an ongoing practice, whereby business leaders define the principles, policies, processes, business rules, and metrics for achieving business objectives, by managing the quality of their master data.

> Challenges regarding master data tend to bedevil most organizations, but it is not always easy to get the right level of business sponsorship to fix the root cause of the issues. As a result, it is important to justify an investment in a master data initiative. For example, consider an organization such as a bank, which is sending multiple pieces of mail to the same household. This bank can establish a quick return on investment by cleansing its customer data to create a single view of "household." The bottom line is that the vast majority of Data Governance programs deal with issues around data stewardship, data quality, master data, and compliance.

11. *Govern analytics.*

Enterprises have invested huge sums of money to build data warehouses to gain competitive insight. However, these investments have not always yielded results; as a consequence, businesses are increasingly scrutinizing their investments in analytics. We define the "Analytics Governance" track as the setting of policies and procedures to better align business users with the investments in analytic infrastructure. Data Governance organizations need to ask the following questions:

- How many users do we have for our data, by business area?
- How many reports do we create, by business area?
- Do the users derive value from these reports?
- How many report executions do we have per month?
- How long does it take to produce a new report?
- What is the cost of producing a new report?
- Can we train the users to produce their own reports?

Many organizations will want to set up a Business Intelligence Competency Center (BICC) to educate users, evangelize business intelligence, and develop reports.

12. *Manage security and privacy.*

Data Governance leaders, especially those who report in to the chief information security officer, often have to deal with issues around data security and privacy. Some of the common data security and privacy challenges include the following:

- Where is our sensitive data?
- Has the organization masked its sensitive data in non-production environments (development, testing, and training) to comply with privacy regulations?
- Are database audit controls in place to prevent privileged users, such as DBAs, from accessing private data, such as employee salaries and customer lists?

13. Govern the information lifecycle.

Unstructured content makes up more than 80 percent of the data within the typical enterprise. As organizations move from Data Governance to Information Governance, they start to consider the governance of this unstructured content.

The lifecycle of information starts with data creation and ends with its removal from production, and shredding from existence. Data Governance organizations have to deal with the following issues regarding the lifecycle of information:

- What is our policy regarding digitizing paper documents?

- What is our records management policy for paper documents, electronic documents, and email? (In other words, which documents do we maintain as records? For how long?)

- How do we archive structured data to reduce storage costs and improve performance?

- How do we bring structured and unstructured data together under a common framework of policies and management?

After these optional tracks, there is one more required step at the end of the Data Governance Unified Process:

14. Measure the results.

Data Governance organizations must ensure continuous improvement by constantly monitoring metrics. In step 9, the Data Governance team sets up the metrics. In this step, the Data Governance team reports on the progress against those metrics to senior stakeholders from IT and the business.

The entire Data Governance Unified Process needs to operate as a continuous loop. The process needs to measure results and loop back to the executive sponsors for the continued endorsement of the Data Governance program.

3

Step 1:
Define the Business Problem

Before we spend a lot of time discussing best practices, it is worth reviewing the key reasons why many Data Governance programs fail. Most organizations with stalled Data Governance programs identify these symptoms:

- "The business does not see any value in Data Governance."

- "The business thinks that IT is responsible for data."

- "The business is focused on near-term objectives, and Data Governance is considered a long-term program."

- "The CIO cut the funding for our Data Governance department."

- "The business reassigned the data stewards to other duties."

When all is said and done, the root cause of failure of Data Governance programs is the lack of linkage to business value. Essentially, IT was governing data without the appropriate business sponsorship. It is not IT's role to govern data. Rather, IT is a custodian that supports, implements, and provides the necessary capabilities to measure and track the data that is leveraged by the business.

The drivers of business value vary by industry, and by company. There is a lot to be said for framing the value of Data Governance in terms the business understands, which goes beyond measuring and managing things of interest to DBAs and business intelligence analysts. Once you frame the value proposition in language used by business executives, you will have engaged executive leaders who have the authority to move mountains, if need be, to achieve improved business benefits from better Data Governance.

Use the examples that follow as a starting point. Of course, ensure that you factor in the unique circumstances of your own industry and organization.

Banking

Within the banking industry, the chief risk officer is emerging as a key business sponsor for the Data Governance program. Credit risk is a great example of how Data Governance can improve the quality of decision-making. Consider the example of a commercial lender that was not able to easily quantify counterparty risk. The lender could not easily quantify the overall exposure to corporate entities with multiple subsidiaries in different countries that had individual lines of credit. The credit risk organization would typically use spreadsheets to calculate counterparty risk, a process that was both time-consuming and error-prone. The senior vice president of credit risk sponsored a solution that included IBM InfoSphere™ Master Data Management coupled with D&B's corporate hierarchies. As a result, the lender was able to make better credit decisions with a faster turnaround time. Several banks now staff full-time data stewardship roles that focus solely on managing corporate and legal hierarchies.

Chief risk officers also have to ensure that their reports can be trusted, always asking the question, "Is the report made up of trusted information?" A Data Governance practitioner at a large bank stated the problem succinctly as follows:

Our chief risk officer is concerned that regulators want to understand the sources of data in our reports. We cannot do that without the appropriate metadata and data lineage, to demonstrate how a specific field in the report is sourced from a particular data mart, which in turn came from the enterprise data warehouse, and ultimately from a set of back-end data sources, with all the data transformations in between.

Security and privacy are also important drivers within the banking industry, with regulations to safeguard personally identifiable information (PII), such as the

Personal Information Protection and Electronic Documents Act (PIPEDA) in Canada. In addition to defining sensitive data, the Data Governance organization at a large financial institution also established a policy that all applications accessing sensitive data fields needed to be approved by the chief privacy officer, or her delegate.

Insurance

The insurance industry tends to have an intense focus on a single view of policyholders and agents to facilitate customer-centric programs, such as cross-selling and up-selling marketing campaigns. For example, a multi-line insurer would like to sell auto insurance and homeowners insurance to all its life-insurance policyholders.

Another example is Solvency II, which is an updated set of regulatory requirements that cover insurance companies operating in the European Union. Solvency II is set to go into effect in late 2012 and has become an area of focus for insurance companies operating in Europe. The objective of Solvency II is to reduce the risk that an insurer would be unable to meet its claims.

Solvency II is sometimes referred to as "Basel II" for insurance companies. Banks faced numerous challenges in sourcing quality data for their Basel II calculations, and it is anticipated that insurers will, as well. The Committee of European Insurance and Occupational Pensions Supervisors (CEIOPS) advises that the quality of Solvency II data should be assessed based on appropriateness, completeness, and accuracy. As a result, European insurers need to be very focused on building out Data Governance programs that are geared toward addressing Solvency II requirements. For example, the Data Governance council might establish a policy that corporate hierarchies need to be properly established to accurately quantify group and counterparty risk.

Retail

Leading-edge retailers are starting to deploy customer-centricity initiatives, including loyalty programs that offer products and even an entire retail experience based on the consumer's wants and needs. Data Governance is especially important as retailers leverage enormous quantities of data to segment their customers. Retailers can also leverage Data Governance best practices to reduce costs. For example, retailers might look to reduce the expense of mailing multiple catalogs to the same household, by matching customers who have a common address. Similarly, the finance and supply chain teams will be interested in a "single view of vendor" to drive down procurement costs and optimize manufacturing rebates. In fact, several retailers have already developed a single view of spend with their top vendors, across multiple divisions and product lines.

The Data Governance organization may establish policies around the format for postal address data required of all customers. It may also write business rules to uniquely identify a "customer" based on specific criteria, such as name and address. It may establish policies around identifying customers that are part of the same household. Finally, the Data Governance organization may reasonably be expected to write a policy and procedure stating that a vendor name must be searched before adding a new one, to minimize duplication.

Government

Several state and local governments are starting to provide a single view of all their services to the citizen. The objective is to allow caseworkers to view a person's family history, financial information, employment background, and eligibility for programs such as food stamps and public healthcare.

Single-view projects in government raise some interesting Data Governance issues. For example, the Data Governance organization must establish policies regarding missing or incomplete address information for the homeless population within the customer information file. In addition, the Data Governance organization at child welfare agencies must establish policies to track unborn children, who do not have a name, address, or social security number. Data Governance organizations must establish policies that address such data anomalies to maximize data sharing and the quality of service for citizens, while minimizing data errors that can cause poor results in myriad government processes. Policies are required around standard naming conventions, rules for handling missing data, and notification rules when potential fraud is discovered.

Government agencies and departments have lots of data about their citizens, including children. The last thing anyone wants is to have this sensitive data fall into the wrong hands. As a result, the Data Governance organization should establish policies around the definition of sensitive data and the mechanism to restrict access on a "need to know" basis.

Healthcare

The healthcare payer and provider industry has to address regulations such as the United States Health Insurance Portability and Accountability Act (HIPAA), which safeguard the security and privacy of *protected health information* (*PHI*). Data Governance plays a key role in identifying PHI data and setting policies to ensure the security and privacy of that data. For example, Data Governance organizations must manage policies and procedures to ensure that patient records are not mixed up, and to preclude adding duplicate patient records. Policies must be established for naming conventions, as well as minimum data requirements for adding new patient records. These policies deal with life-and-death issues, and the Data Governance organization is the only group with the authority to marshal the resources required to guarantee consistent levels of data quality for patient safety, privacy, and security.

Data Governance also plays a pivotal role in ensuring that health plans have a single view of their members, providers, and brokers. Health plans currently have a number of siloed systems, in which it is not uncommon for new-member information to be entered on ten different screens. As a result, the member information is inconsistent and scattered around the health plan's systems. The Data Governance organization needs to set policies around the definition of "member" across the enterprise. It also needs to provide a single mechanism to update changes to data such as name and address across all of the siloed systems. With the appropriate implementation of Data Governance policies, health plans can reduce the cost and effort to administer these fragmented systems.

Telecommunications

A number of telecommunications service providers ("telcos") have grown through mergers and acquisitions. In the United States, the telcos historically evolved as monopoly organizations mandated by the Public Utilities Commission (PUC). Over time, the individual, state-specific organizations merged into organizations representing groups of states. For example, Pacific Northwest Bell was formed from two states (Washington and Oregon). At the time of the AT&T divestiture, these Bell Operating Companies were merged to form Regional Bell Operating Companies (RBOCs). For example, Pacific Northwest Bell merged with Mountain Bell and Northwestern Bell to form US WEST. Eventually, the regional companies, such as BellSouth, Ameritech, and Pacific Bell, were acquired by national carriers.

The state PUCs governed the products offered in each state. Each RBOC invested in its own ordering and billing systems, with specific standards and formats for product data encoded in Universal Service Order Codes (USOCs) and Field Identifiers (FIDs). To offer a standard product for the enterprise, a product manager had to traverse through three levels of data standards: enterprise, regional, and state. In addition, the ordering and billing systems had their own standards for product data and rules.

The impact of all this complexity is seen in such issues as long training time for call center representatives and long lead times for introducing new products, bundles, and promotions (as each product change has to be translated to each state, region, or application). As the telcos start to re-engineer their ordering and billing systems to provide a more flexible environment for product introduction, these product codes and rules must be placed under common Data Governance across regions, states, and applications. The benefits to the organization are enormous, as a standard product offers a far better brand image, faster time to market, reduced training time for call center representatives, and simpler self-service web interfaces.

The telcos are also increasingly concerned about their data growth. With an overall decline in pricing, data communication is rapidly growing without any corresponding increase in revenue. At the same time, there are significant regulatory constraints on data retention. The result is that CIOs are seeing runaway storage costs eating into the rest of the IT budget. A number of telcos are embracing data archiving in a multi-tiered storage environment to reduce overall storage cost, by replacing online storage with offline disk or tape storage. However, applying an archival policy consistently in a fragmented information environment is difficult. The archival policies are best adapted at the business object level. For example, suppose that the data associated with a specific customer needs to be held in primary storage, due to a legal dispute. This data must be managed across all of the business objects—customer data, order data, inventory data, network events, and so on. In a fragmented environment, without Data Governance, it is difficult, if not impossible, to isolate specific tables and columns in ordering and billing systems or data warehouses and relate them to specific business objects. Data Governance provides the discipline to establish enterprise-wide definitions of business objects, which traverse business functions, geographic regions, and acquired entities.

Finally, the typical telco has billing systems and subscriber data that are oriented by product offering, such as landline, DSL, and wireless. As a result, it is very hard to run marketing campaigns that offer customers a discount for using more than one service. Data Governance organizations need to establish policies to match subscriber names across multiple systems as telcos become more customer-centric and less product-centric in their operations.

Manufacturers with Large ERP Implementations

Manufacturers with Enterprise Resource Planning (ERP) implementations such as SAP or Oracle face significant challenges around Data Governance. Even the most extensive ERP implementation will not cover the entire enterprise. As a result, enterprises continue to retain a significant amount of their data outside their ERP environments. Many companies have multiple ERP instances for different business units, functions, and geographic regions. The bottom line is that enterprise data tends to be fragmented.

Enterprises with large ERP implementations need to consider a number of aspects of Data Governance:

- *Data quality*—Data quality is about having data that is "fit for purpose." Each data field does not need to be complete or accurate; rather, it only has to be accurate within the context in which it is being used. Poor data quality is the main cause of failure of any large ERP implementation. Experienced practitioners agree that data integration consumes about 40 percent of the cost of a typical ERP implementation.

  Because it is extremely difficult to delete data once it is loaded into an ERP application, special care must be given to the quality of data added to a new environment. We often see organizations that spend millions of dollars to implement a data quality program on a one-time basis, but do not persist with their data quality efforts. The quality of data at these organizations goes backwards over time. Organizations need to put plans in place to monitor the quality of data continuously over time, to ensure quality standards are both met and continued.

- *Master data management*—ERP implementations require a system of record (SOR) for key entities such as customer, vendor, bill of materials, product, and chart of accounts. Enterprises should appoint data stewards who will ensure that the data is "fit for purpose." For example, customer data needs to address the needs of sales, customer service, and marketing. Vendor data needs to serve the procurement and supply-chain areas, while product data is the focus of the R&D organization. The Data Governance organization must write policies to maximize the re-use of shared data across the enterprise. For example, it might establish a policy stating that a certain geocoding format is used across the enterprise, to ensure that marketing and ERP applications work together seamlessly.

- *Information lifecycle governance*—The cost of storage is a significant driver for enterprises that look to archive data, whether that data is structured, unstructured (such as vendor invoices), or a combination of both. In addition, archiving significantly improves the performance of the application, by reducing the amount of data in the production environment and therefore speeding access to the data.

- *Security and privacy*—Enterprises need to comply with privacy regulations by masking sensitive data such as national identifiers and employee salaries. This needs to occur in non-production environments such as development, testing, and training, as well as in production environments. This requirement is even more important when data is shipped externally, such as to an outsourcer.

- *Metadata management*—It is important to have a data dictionary or business glossary to ensure that business terms are interpreted correctly by both business and IT. For example, the term "landed cost" could mean "landed cost at store," "landed cost at port," or "landed cost at distributor." All these definitions might be correct, so it is important to provide the definition in context. A sound metadata layer is also important to enable *data lineage*, the ability to track data all the way from a report back to the source.

4

Step 2:
Obtain Executive Sponsorship

A
s with any project, it is important to have the right level of executive sponsorship for the Data Governance program. Step 2 of the IBM Data Governance Unified Process addresses this, with the following typical questions:

- Should Data Governance be "owned" by IT or the business?

- How can we leverage existing grassroots Data Governance initiatives?

- What level of the organization should be involved in Data Governance?

Here are the sub-steps associated with obtaining executive sponsorship:

2.1 Create a virtual Data Governance working team.

2.2 Obtain support from senior management within IT and the business.

2.3 Identify an owner for Data Governance.

Let's walk through each sub-step in further detail.

2.1 Create a Virtual Data Governance Working Team

As with any major endeavor, Data Governance rarely starts as a top-down initiative. Rather, it begins with a few like-minded individuals within an organization who are focused on a better way to manage data. For example, the Data Governance organization at a large manufacturer was started by a group of individuals from the data architecture, risk management, records management, business intelligence, stewardship, and finance groups. These people reported into different parts of the organization, but they were all grappling with similar issues around data.

The data architecture team wanted better alignment between IT and the business. Risk management wanted better policies around data privacy. The records management team wanted to establish retention policies for electronic documents. The business intelligence and finance teams were working through data quality issues in enterprise reporting. Finally, the chief data steward wanted to ensure that the business provided the right level of sponsorship to the entire stewardship program. This group started meeting on a biweekly basis. Over time, they established a Data Governance working group.

2.2 Obtain Support from Senior Management Within IT and the Business

Corporate governance provides a useful analogy to explain the importance of engaging stakeholders early and often in the Data Governance process. At the pinnacle of corporate governance is the board of directors, which represents the interests of the shareholders. The board of directors is responsible for setting policies that ensure appropriate governance by the executive officers of the corporation. Similarly, Data Governance will succeed only if the process engages the right stakeholders from IT and the business.

The process of stakeholder identification is very important. As a general rule, any function that relies on data for effective performance is a stakeholder. In most organizations, the IT organization will be engaged, especially if it includes teams focused on data architecture and business intelligence. The chief marketing officer often leads with the most "skin in the game" for managing customer data across the enterprise. Finance, likewise, is often a key stakeholder. The chief information security officer (CISO) may also be engaged, along with representatives from key business units. Finally, there are certain key functions that will want to participate in the Data Governance process. These functions vary by industry; they include marketing, finance, and risk management in banking; actuarial, underwriting, and claims in insurance; and supply chain in manufacturing.

The Data Governance process needs to engage these stakeholders by laying out the benefits associated with sound Data Governance. Chapter 11, on metrics, discusses this topic in greater detail.

2.3 Identify an Owner for Data Governance

We could have placed this sub-step under step 5, "Establish the Organizational Blueprint," instead of here in step 2. However, we wanted to highlight the importance of identifying an owner early in the Data Governance process. As with anything of importance, it is critical to have accountability to ensure the successful implementation of a Data Governance program.

Because data is the lifeblood of a business, ownership of Data Governance can be fraught with political issues within an organization. In many cases, ownership of Data Governance tends to be with whomever is most passionate about the topic or has the first-mover advantage. Notwithstanding this, there are multiple ways to identify an appropriate owner for Data Governance:

- *By organization*—Data Governance might be organized as a corporate function; or it might be owned by a specific line of business, multiple lines of business; or both. The advantage of Data Governance as a corporate function is that there will be some consistency in the Data Governance program across the enterprise. The disadvantage is that Data Governance might be perceived as being too far removed from the needs of the lines of business.

  Having a line of business own Data Governance improves the odds that the program will be tightly linked to the business. However, there is a risk that multiple lines of business will develop their own Data Governance programs. This approach also makes it more difficult to implement enterprise-wide initiatives, such as Master Data Management. As a compromise, some type of hybrid approach, with both corporate and line-of-business participation, works in many organizations.

- *By function*—A few key functions tend to own Data Governance in most organizations:

  » *Security*—During the early years, Data Governance was dominated by security and privacy, with the chief information security officer being the primary sponsor for the initiative. Over the past few years, ownership of the Data Governance program by the CISO has been on the decline, although security and privacy are still important parts of the initiative.

  » *Risk*—The chief risk officer is emerging as a key sponsor for some Data Governance programs, especially within banks. The global financial crisis has convinced banks that they need trusted data to support sound risk management.

  » *Marketing*—The chief marketing officer is continually seeking new sources of external and internal data to gain further insight into customer behavior and competitive intelligence. The globalization of many industries provides new challenges in accessing and governing the disparate data, such as currency, language, and customs, needed to understand new markets and the threats of foreign competition.

  » *Other functional domains*—This often varies by industry. For example, the drilling function and the vice president of drilling would be responsible for well data within an oil and gas company.

  » *Information Technology*—Over the past few years, ownership of Data Governance by the chief information officer (CIO) and the IT organization is on the rise. The downside to this approach is that the business, not IT, is in the best position to define rules and policies for Data Governance.

Here are the roles that tend to lead Data Governance within IT:

- Enterprise data architect
- Manager, program manager, director, or vice president of information management
- Manager, program manager, director, or vice president of business intelligence

The enterprise data warehouse tends to be the lightning rod for Data Governance issues, because of all the challenges associated with data quality and the lack of trusted information. Think back to the many warehouse projects of the late 1990s that failed. Why did they fail? The data got into the warehouse, and the reports were available. However, the quality of data was often poor, so the business that depended on the data had bad experiences, and therefore negative impressions. It was a classic example of "garbage in, garbage out."

To move forward, new data warehouse projects are looking to change prior experiences from negative to positive by implementing governance processes to improve the quality of the data. A common lament from the business intelligence team is that there "are multiple reports going to senior management that all have inconsistent data." Having said that, it is much more effective to govern data early, at the source, rather than late, at the data warehouse.

Many organizations have part-time owners of Data Governance who perform other functions as well, including enterprise data architecture, risk management, and corporate security. However, full-time Data Governance positions are increasingly being staffed, as organizations recognize the value of data as an enterprise asset. Appendix C shows an example of a job posting for a Data Governance officer. The job posting has a focus on data quality, data stewardship, metrics, reporting results, and alignment with the business.

5

Step 3:
Conduct the Maturity Assessment

Wa e begin this chapter with a general discussion of maturity models. Developed by the Software Engineering Institute (SEI) in 1984, the Capability Maturity Model (CMM) is a methodology used to develop and refine an organization's software development process. The CMM describes a five-level, graduated path, shown in Figure 5.1. This path provides a framework

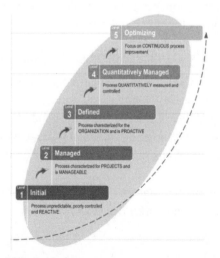

Figure 5.1: The Capability Maturity Model.

for prioritizing actions, a starting point, a common language, and a methodology to measure progress. Ultimately, this structured collection of elements offers a steady, measurable progression to the final desired maturity state.

At Maturity Level 1 (initial), processes are usually ad hoc, and the environment is not stable. Success reflects the competence of individuals within the organization, rather than the use of proven processes. While organizations at Level 1 often produce products and services that work, they frequently exceed their budget and project schedule.

At Maturity Level 2 (managed), successes are repeatable, but the processes might not repeat for all projects in the organization. Basic project management helps track costs and schedules, while process discipline helps ensure that existing practices are retained. When these practices are in place, projects are performed and managed according to their documented plans. There is still a risk, however, of exceeding cost and time estimates.

At Maturity Level 3 (defined), the organization's set of standard processes are used to establish consistency across the organization. The standards, process descriptions, and procedures for a project are tailored from the organization's set of standard processes, to suit a particular project or organizational unit.

At Maturity Level 4 (quantitatively managed), organizations set quantitative quality goals for both process and maintenance. Selected sub-processes significantly contribute to overall process performance and are controlled using statistical and other quantitative techniques.

Finally, at Maturity Level 5 (optimizing), quantitative process improvement objectives for the organization are firmly established and continually revised to reflect changing business objectives and are used as criteria in managing process improvement.

The IBM Data Governance Maturity Model is an important step forward because it helps to educate other stakeholders about how they can help make the strategy more effective. Developed based on input from the members of the IBM Data Governance Council, the Maturity Model defines the scope of who needs to be involved in governing and measuring the way businesses govern data—for example, sensitive customer information or financial details—across an organization.

The IBM Data Governance Maturity Model measures Data Governance competencies based on 11 categories of Data Governance maturity, shown in Figure 5.2.

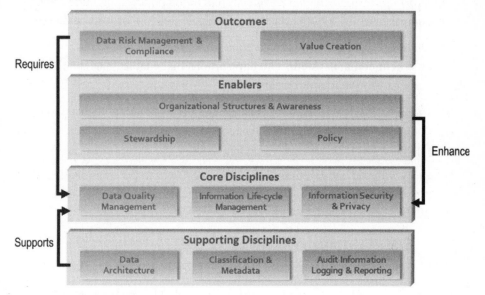

Figure 5.2: The IBM Data Governance Maturity Model.

1. *Data Risk Management and Compliance* is a methodology by which risks are identified, qualified, quantified, avoided, accepted, mitigated, or transferred out.

2. *Value Creation* is a process by which data assets are qualified and quantified to enable the business to maximize the value created by data assets.

3. *Organizational Structures and Awareness* refers to the level of mutual responsibility between business and IT, and the recognition of fiduciary responsibility to govern data at different levels of management.

4. *Stewardship* is a quality-control discipline designed to ensure the custodial care of data for asset enhancement, risk mitigation, and organizational control.

5. *Policy* is the written articulation of desired organizational behavior.

6. *Data Quality Management* refers to methods to measure, improve, and certify the quality and integrity of production, test, and archival data.

7. *Information Lifecycle Management* is a systematic, policy-based approach to information collection, use, retention, and deletion.

8. *Information Security and Privacy* refers to the policies, practices, and controls used by an organization to mitigate risk and protect data assets.

9. *Data Architecture* is the architectural design of structured and unstructured data systems and applications that enables data availability and distribution to appropriate users.

10. *Classification and Metadata* refers to the methods and tools used to create common semantic definitions for business and IT terms, data models, and repositories.

11. *Audit Information Logging and Reporting* refers to the organizational processes for monitoring and measuring the data value, risks, and effectiveness of data governance.

These 11 categories of Data Governance can be divided into four inter-related groupings:

- *Outcomes* are the anticipated results of the Data Governance program. These tend to be focused on reducing risk and increasing value, which are in turn driven by reducing costs and increasing revenues.

- *Enablers* include the areas of Organizational Structures and Awareness, Policy, and Stewardship.

- *Core disciplines* include Data Quality Management, Information Lifecycle Management, and Information Security and Privacy.

- *Supporting disciplines* including Data Architecture, Classification and Metadata, and Audit Information Logging and Reporting.

These categories are tightly intertwined. For example, an organization might want to focus on Value Creation as an outcome of its Data Governance program, based on cross-selling and up-selling to existing customers. The enterprise will look to deploy Data Stewardship roles to improve the quality of its customer data. The enterprise will also look to implement an enterprise Master Data Management program with an SOR for "customer." Finally, the enterprise will need to set up a Data Governance organization to drive the initiative, and to set policies around the definition of customer attributes and the sharing of customer data across organizational boundaries.

You can only start to address an issue if you first acknowledge that you have one. The best way to kick-start Data Governance is to conduct an assessment along the following lines:

- Current state: where are we today?

- Future state: where would we like to be in the future?

- Roadmap: what people, process, technology, and policy initiatives do we need to bridge the gap between the current and future states?

Figure 5.3 provides a sample of the gaps between the current and future states using the framework of the IBM Data Governance Maturity Model. The levels of maturity map directly to the Capability Maturity Model. The best way to conduct a Data Governance maturity assessment is to conduct a workshop with the right participants from IT and the business.

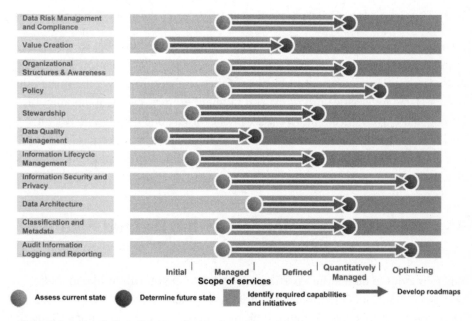

Figure 5.3: A sample Data Governance maturity assessment.

Here are the detailed sub-steps involved in conducting a Data Governance maturity assessment:

3.1 Define the organizational scope of the assessment.

3.2 Define the time horizon for the desired future state of Data Governance.

3.3 Define the Data Governance categories to be assessed.

3.4 Identify the right participants from business and IT for the workshop.

3.5 Conduct the Data Governance maturity assessment workshop.

3.6 Socialize the results of the assessment with senior executives.

The rest of this chapter provides detailed discussions of these sub-steps.

3.1 Define the Organizational Scope of the Assessment

Except at the very smallest of companies, it might not be possible to assign one rating for the entire enterprise. Even in the case of small companies, there might be one particular department or business function that will derive the most value from a Data Governance program. You might, therefore, decide to conduct the initial Data Governance maturity assessment for just one geographic region, business unit, or function, such as supply chain or sales. At the end of the day, it is all about "internal selling" of the Data Governance program to the key stakeholders.

3.2 Define the Time Horizon for the Desired Future State of Data Governance

It is important to define the timeframe within which you would like to make changes to the Data Governance maturity assessment. This timeframe should not be so short that it is very difficult to produce meaningful change, nor so long that the organization loses focus due to lack of tangible results.

Most organizations tend to pick a time period of 12 to 18 months. For example, a bank might decide to focus exclusively on the risk function for the Data Governance maturity assessment. Having made that decision, the bank might well determine that it needs to make the desired changes to the Data

Governance maturity assessment within a period of 18 months. As a result, the bank might then have to decide how to move the risk function from an assessment of "1" to "3" for the Classification and Metadata competency within 18 months. From a value-creation perspective, the risk team will want to be able to leverage improved metadata capabilities to demonstrate data lineage for key regulatory reports.

3.3 Define the Data Governance Categories to Be Assessed

Depending on the appetite for Data Governance within your organization, you will probably decide to start with only a subset of the categories of the IBM Data Governance Maturity Model. For example, you might decide to focus on only one division within your enterprise. As a result, you might decide that the Security and Privacy competency is out of scope for the assessment, because that function is handled by corporate. Or, it might turn out that your Data Governance program needs to be more focused on structured data, so any discussions around records management and unstructured content will be out of scope with regard to the Information Lifecycle Management competency.

3.4 Identify the Right Participants from Business and IT for the Workshop

A good mix of business and IT is an essential prerequisite to conducting a sound Data Governance maturity assessment. There is no correct list of functions and departments, but you need to ensure the right participants to maximize the chances of obtaining the appropriate buy-in to any recommendations from the workshop.

The typical IT participants might include the information management team, the business intelligence and data warehousing leaders, the enterprise data architect, the records management team, and security and privacy professionals. The business participants might include representatives from sales, finance, marketing, risk, and other relevant job functions or divisions that rely on data for effective performance. Typical roles from this group of participants include those setting policy, performing analysis, generating reports, developing models, engineering business processes, and managing data stewardship.

3.5 Conduct the Data Governance Maturity Assessment Workshop

Once you have scoped out the Data Governance maturity assessment, it is time to conduct the workshop. The duration of the workshop may vary from a couple of days to several weeks, depending on the needs of the organization. In many cases, an organization may decide to bring the key stakeholders together for a one- or two-day workshop, followed by a series of interviews with key stakeholders.

3.6 Socialize the Results of the Assessment with Senior Executives

Once you have completed the Data Governance maturity assessment, it is important to share the results with key IT and business stakeholders. That way, you can start to build an organizational consensus about the key problems, such as lack of organizational alignment, metadata, and data quality. You can also help the senior leaders begin the process of generating buy-in and ownership of the potential next steps. We will discuss the process of building a roadmap in the next chapter.

Appendix D includes a sample questionnaire for a Data Governance maturity assessment.

6

Step 4:
Build a Roadmap

Three sub-tasks facilitate the development of a Data Governance roadmap:

    4.1 Summarize the results of the Data Governance maturity assessment.

    4.2 List the key people, process, and technology initiatives necessary to bridge the gaps highlighted in the assessment.

    4.3 Create a roadmap based on a prioritization of key initiatives.

4.1 Summarize the Results of the Data Governance Maturity Assessment

Once you have completed an assessment of Data Governance maturity, you will have three data points for each category that you have assessed:

- An assessment of the current state (low = 1, high = 5)

- An assessment of the desired future state (low = 1, high = 5)

- The delta between the current state and the desired future state

It is important to recognize that a "1" rating is not inherently bad, and a "5" rating is not necessarily good. The Data Governance organization has to work with IT and business stakeholders and (preferably) develop a business case to determine whether it is feasible to increase the rating for a given category in the desired future state.

4.2 List the Key People, Process, and Technology Initiatives Necessary to Bridge the Gaps

Figure 6.1 shows an example of a bank that has established a Data Governance program focused on customer-centricity, with marketing as a key sponsor. The bank would like to increase its share of wallet by increasing the number of products it sells to each retail customer. The bank's marketing department has determined that its retail customers generally have only one account with the bank—either a checking account or a mortgage.

People	Process	Technology
• Establish a Data Governance council focused on customer-centricity • Include senior leaders from retail banking, finance, marketing, and IT within the Data Governance council • Appoint stewards for customer, account, and product data	• Make declarations about principles, policies, procedures, business rules, and metrics • Develop a Data Governance charter • Build a business case for customer-centric Data Governance • Define metrics to monitor execution of the Data Governance program	• Implement a transactional-style Master Data Management hub as the system of record (SOR) for customer, account, and product data • Discover existing data sources • Define attributes for the SOR • Map data sources to the MDM hub

Figure 6.1: A list of key Data Governance initiatives for a bank.

The bank has decided to implement a series of people, process, and technology initiatives around Data Governance.

On the people side, the bank needs to establish a Data Governance council focused on customer-centricity as a near-term business objective. The bank has prioritized customer, account, and product as the key data domains. Accordingly, the Data Governance council needs to include membership from the retail banking, finance, and marketing areas as key business sponsors, in addition to IT. The bank also needs to appoint stewards within retail banking to oversee these data domains, and to manage data quality on an ongoing basis.

On the process side, the Data Governance organization needs to make declarations of principles, policies, procedures, business rules, and metrics. (See Appendix E for more information about Data Governance declarations.) It must adopt a charter that is focused on customer-centricity, and it must establish key metrics, such as the number of products per customer. It also needs to develop a business case, to justify the overall program.

Finally, on the technology side, the Data Governance program needs to oversee the implementation of a Master Data Management (MDM) hub that will be the system of record (SOR) for customer, account, and product data. The Data Governance program needs to discover existing sources of data, define the attributes of the master data, and map the data models of the source systems into the MDM hub.

4.3 Create a Roadmap Based on a Prioritization of Key Initiatives

Figure 6.2 shows a roadmap for the Data Governance initiative, based on an 18-month timeline to demonstrate initial results. The Data Governance process

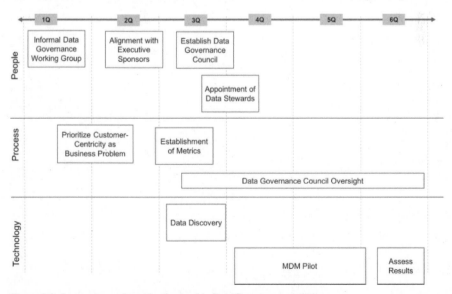

Figure 6.2: A sample roadmap for the bank's Data Governance initiatives.

at the bank starts with the formation of an informal Data Governance working group, consisting of mid-level managers from key functional areas such as retail banking, finance, marketing, and IT. Given the fragmentation of customer data across multiple data sources, the marketing and retail banking teams will prioritize customer-centricity as the key business problem for the Data Governance program. The bank must realistically devote two quarters to properly complete the process of executive alignment.

Over the next two quarters, the Data Governance council will be formally established, data stewards will be appointed, and key metrics will be agreed upon. At the same time, the Data Governance team will discover existing sources of data and agree upon the SOR's attributes. The MDM pilot will be kicked off during the fourth quarter and will continue for two more quarters.

Finally, the bank should be able to assess the results of the program within 18 months. The entire process will be under the oversight of the Data Governance council.

7

Step 5:
Establish the Organizational
Blueprint

S tep 5 of the IBM Data Governance Unified Process defines the best way to organize a Data Governance program for maximum results. Here are this step's key sub-steps:

5.1   Define the Data Governance charter.

5.2   Define the organizational structure for Data Governance.

5.3   Establish the Data Governance council.

5.4   Establish the Data Governance working group.

5.5   Identify data stewards.

5.6   Conduct regular meetings of the Data Governance council and working group.

Each of these sub-steps is discussed in a section below.

5.1 Define the Data Governance Charter

The Data Governance charter is similar to the Articles of Incorporation of a corporation. The charter spells out the primary objectives of the program and its key stakeholders, as well as roles and responsibilities, decision rights, and measures of success. Appendix B provides a sample Data Governance charter.

5.2 Define the Organizational Structure for Data Governance

The optimal organization for Data Governance is a three-tier structure. The Data Governance council, at the pinnacle of the organization, includes senior stakeholders. At the next level down, the Data Governance working group consists of members who are responsible for governing data on a fairly regular basis. Finally, the data stewardship community has day-to-day, hands-on responsibility for data.

5.3 Establish the Data Governance Council

The Data Governance council consists of the executive sponsors for the program. The council defines the Data Governance vision and goals, provides alignment within the organization across business and IT, sets the overall direction for the Data Governance program, and acts as a tiebreaker in disagreements over policy.

Depending on the outcomes expected from the program, the Data Governance council will be chaired by the chief information officer, the vice president of information management, the chief information security officer, or the chief risk officer. This council will also include functional representation from the finance, legal, and HR teams, as well as representatives from various lines of business that have a stake in data as an enterprise asset. These executives are the overall champions for the Data Governance program and ensure buy-in across the organization.

5.4 Establish the Data Governance Working Group

The Data Governance working group is the next level down from the council in the organization. The working group runs the Data Governance program on a day-to-day basis. It is also responsible for oversight of the data stewardship community.

The Data Governance working group is chaired by the Data Governance leader. While this leader may also have another role within the data architecture, information security, or risk group, many organizations are now appointing full-time managers and directors of Data Governance.

5.5 Identify Data Stewards

Data stewards ideally report into the business and have a custodial role for data. Data stewards address specific issues and concerns on a day-to-day basis and define data within and across the organization. (This topic is covered in much greater detail in Chapter 12.)

5.6 Conduct Regular Meetings of the Data Governance Council and Working Group

The Data Governance council meets to set Data Governance policies and to track the performance of the Data Governance program. The council, which includes senior leadership, meets regularly, but not necessarily frequently. Typical council meetings are scheduled on a monthly or quarterly basis and last for one to two hours.

Sample topics on the agenda of a Data Governance council meeting include the following:

- Review the Data Governance scorecard. (This topic is covered in further detail in Chapter 11.)

- Sign off on the records management strategy, including document classification, retention schedules, and electronic discovery (eDiscovery).

- In conjunction with the chief information security officer, sign off on the policy to discover and secure hidden PII.

- Agree on the overall executive sponsor for customer and product data.

The Data Governance working group includes middle management. It meets more frequently, typically on a biweekly basis. Working group meetings might last three or four hours, depending on the urgency of specific initiatives.

Here are some sample topics on the agenda of a Data Governance working group meeting:

- Agree on the attributes of the SOR for "customer."
- Agree on the process when two divisions have the ability to update the same attribute.
- Create business rules to match, merge, and link related customer records.
- In conjunction with the legal department, review the eDiscovery process.

Figure 7.1 describes a sample Data Governance organization at a manufacturer. This manufacturer has adopted a three-tier Data Governance organization, with a council, a working group, and data stewards. The Data Governance council is chaired by the chief information officer. The council also includes key functional stakeholders such as the chief financial officer, the chief risk officer, and the senior vice president of the supply chain group. Finally, the heads of key business units are also members of the council.

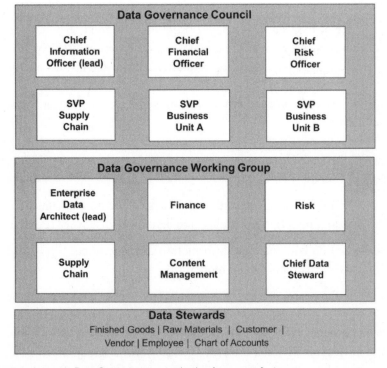

Figure 7.1: A sample Data Governance organization for a manufacturer.

At the next level down, the Data Governance working group is chaired by the enterprise data architect, who sets the agenda for the group and leads the meetings. The working group also includes stakeholders from the finance, risk and supply chain areas. The working group also includes a member from the content management area, given the importance of governance of unstructured data. The chief data steward, who oversees the data stewardship program, is also a member of the Data Governance working group.

The data stewardship community consists of data stewards who are responsible for key subject areas. The stewards for finished goods, raw materials, and vendor data report into the supply chain group. The steward for customer data reports into sales. The steward for employee data reports into human resources. Finally, the data steward for the chart of accounts reports into finance.

Figure 7.2 describes a sample Data Governance organization at a mid-sized bank. This bank has also adopted a three-tier Data Governance organization, with a council, a working group, and data stewards.

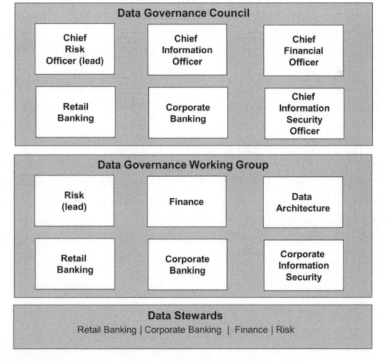

Figure 7.2: A sample Data Governance organization for a mid-sized bank.

The bank's Data Governance council is chaired by the chief risk officer because of the intense focus on improving the quality of risk data. The Data Governance council also includes key functional stakeholders such as the chief information officer, the chief financial officer, and the chief information security officer. Finally, the heads of the retail banking and corporate banking units are also members of the council.

At the next level down, the Data Governance working group is chaired by the vice president of risk, who sets the agenda for the group and leads the meetings. The working group also includes stakeholders from the finance, data architecture, and security areas. The group also includes mid-level representatives from retail banking and corporate banking.

The bank has adopted a hybrid form of data stewardship by organization and functional area. The bank has data stewards within retail banking, commercial banking, finance, and risk, who perform quality control on a part-time basis. In addition, the bank is piloting a Master Data Management initiative around customer data for both retail and corporate banking.

Within retail banking, the data stewards are responsible for identifying all the customer relationships with the bank across multiple products, such as checking accounts, mortgages, and credit cards. These relationships need to be identified not just at the individual level, but also at the household level. For example, if Mr. Smith and Mrs. Smith both have accounts at the bank, they need to be captured in a single view.

Within corporate banking, the data stewards are responsible for maintaining legal hierarchies. They will use tools such as D&B D-U-N-S Numbers, which are unique nine-digit sequences to identify millions of businesses worldwide. The D&B D-U-N-S Numbers will allow data stewards to ensure that two companies that are part of the same corporate group will be included within the same legal hierarchy. The finance data steward is responsible for ensuring the quality of financial data. Similarly, the risk data steward is responsible for ensuring the quality of data being used for risk calculations.

8

Step 6:
Build a Data Dictionary

One department in an organization refers to "revenue," while another refers to "sales." Are both departments referring to the same activity? One subsidiary talks about "customers," another about "users" or "clients." Are these different classifications, or different terms for the same classification?

Business metadata relates to the definition of business terms. Business metadata is critical for end users of information. It allows these end users to be confident that the data they rely on for making business decisions is exactly what they expected. Effective management of business metadata ensures that the same descriptive language applies throughout the organization.

A data dictionary, or *business glossary*, is a repository with definitions of key terms that bring together common definitions across business and IT. Organizations deploy data dictionaries to ensure that business terms are well-defined in context. However, to be effective, the data dictionary needs to be populated with business terms that have been agreed to by the relevant business areas.

Many organizations wrestle with the inconsistency of business terms across the enterprise. This inconsistency might be caused by events such as mergers and acquisitions, or by systemic, siloed approaches to the definition of a common business vocabulary. The root cause is often attributed to the absence of an effective Data Governance and stewardship program.

There are eight key sub-steps involved in building a data dictionary:

6.1 Select a data domain.

6.2 Assign data stewards to maintain key business terms.

6.3 Identify critical data elements.

6.4 Jumpstart the data dictionary with an existing glossary of terms.

6.5 Populate the data dictionary.

6.6 Link business terms with technical artifacts.

6.7 Support Data Governance auditing, reporting, and logging requirements.

6.8 Integrate the data dictionary with the application environment.

The rest of this chapter walks through these sub-steps in greater detail.

6.1 Select a Data Domain

The organization needs to pick a data domain, such as risk or finance. The best practice is to pick a domain that has a lot of issues around data definitions and is willing to work with the Data Governance program around the development of a data dictionary.

6.2 Assign Data Stewards to Maintain Key Business Terms

Once the data domain has been selected, the Data Governance organization needs to ensure that stewards are assigned to groups of related terms. These stewards will be responsible for the ongoing maintenance of the definitions and for ensuring the appropriate alignment between business and IT. Figure 8.1 shows an example of data stewardship within IBM InfoSphere Business Glossary. In this example, Scott Montgomery has been assigned as a steward. We can view all the assets that he manages, as well as his organization and contact information.

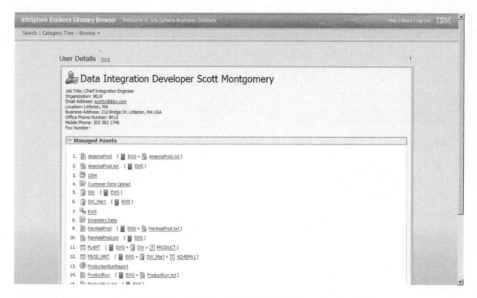

Figure 8.1: An example of data stewardship within IBM InfoSphere Business Glossary.

6.3 Identify Critical Data Elements

In identifying critical data elements, let's consider an example that is relevant to every organization. The hypothetical Company ABC has a report that says it has 250,000 customers. The issue, however, is how do you define the term "customer"? Marketing might define it to include prospects. Sales might define it to include parties that have an opportunity in the CRM system. Finance might only want to include parties that have purchased a product within the past 12 months. Finally, do you count a multinational with multiple subsidiaries as one customer or several?

Figure 8.2 shows the definitions for "high value customer" that have been recorded by the data steward within IBM InfoSphere Business Glossary. The glossary not only displays the current definition of the term but also the previous definitions and the names of the people who made changes to the definition.

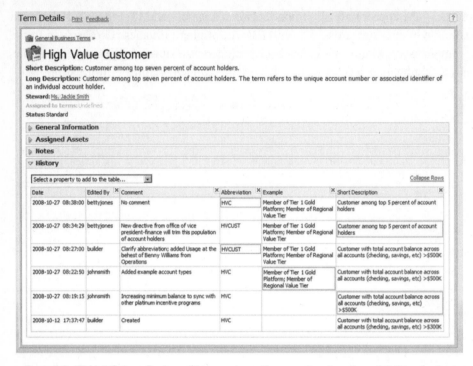

Figure 8.2: IBM InfoSphere Business Glossary shows the current and previous definitions for the term "high value customer."

As you can see in the example, the term "high value customer" refers to any customer among the top seven percent of account holders. However, the term had several other definitions in the past, including any customer with a balance across all accounts (checking, savings, and so on) exceeding $300K.

A European telecommunications service provider had first-hand experience with this challenge, when different functional areas within the organization could not agree on a consistent definition for the term "active subscriber." For example, the billing department defined an active subscriber as someone who had received a bill in the previous 30 days. The network department defined an active subscriber as someone who had used the carrier's network in the previous 30 days. The key difference between these two definitions related to subscribers who had signed up for service but who had switched SIM cards and were roaming outside the carrier's network on a full-time basis.

The Data Governance team was able to establish a consistent set of definitions in this case. It got people out of their silos to share information and see the broader business concepts and drivers. The Data Governance organization then re-used these common definitions across others parts of the organization, as well.

6.4 Jumpstart the Data Dictionary with an Existing Glossary of Terms

IBM InfoSphere Business Glossary provides an easy-to-use, web-based user interface for creating, managing, and sharing a controlled vocabulary. There are IBM InfoSphere Business Glossary packs for the telecommunications, financial services, retail, insurance, and healthcare industries. These packs provide rich industry content to jumpstart a glossary project. An organization can then customize these glossaries to meet its specific needs.

6.5 Populate the Data Dictionary

The next sub-step is to populate the data dictionary with the agreed-upon business terms. IBM InfoSphere Business Glossary provides a web-based portal for the definition, management, search, and exploration of business vocabulary and its rules and relationships. From IBM InfoSphere Business Glossary's entry page, a business user can use either the category tree or the search capabilities to find information. Categories can be defined based on business classification schemes such as "Finance," "Human Resources," and "Products," or based on geographies and locations.

Figure 8.3 shows an example of the category tree view of terms within IBM InfoSphere Business Glossary. In this example, the term "high value customer" is listed under "customer interaction analysis."

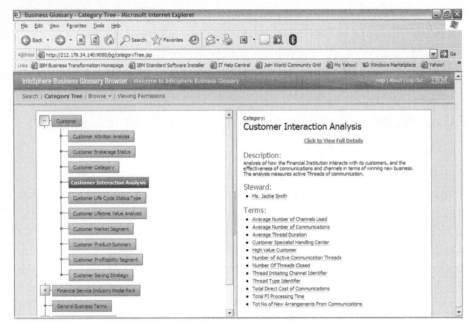

Figure 8.3: IBM InfoSphere Business Glossary's category tree.

A business user can also use IBM InfoSphere Business Glossary Browser to search and explore the meanings defined in the glossary. An example of this is shown in Figure 8.4.

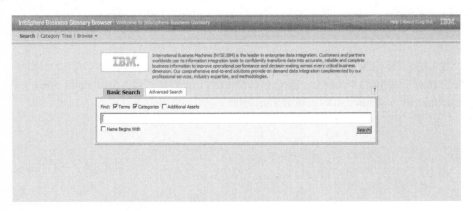

Figure 8.4: IBM InfoSphere Business Glossary Browser.

6.6 Link Business Terms with Technical Artifacts

As described in the white paper *The Business Value of a Business Glossary* (IBM Software Group and Lowell Fryman, October 2008), once business definitions are agreed upon, the data architects need to establish linkages between the terms and technical artifacts such as database tables and columns. For example, the data architect might link the term "vendor" to the SUPPLIER table in the database and link the term "vendor number" to the SUPP_NUM column in the SUPPLIER table. These linkages help establish two-way communication between business and IT, which facilitates effective Data Governance.

Business users can drill down from a term to find the technical data sources. At the same time, technical users working on a data source or ETL job, or creating a business report, can understand the business context of the data being used.

6.7 Support Data Governance Auditing, Reporting, and Logging Requirements

Business terminology is always subject to change. What defines a "high value customer" today might be different tomorrow. As business requirements evolve, so might the acceptable definition of a term. Being able to see the history of what changed, why it changed, and who changed it is as important as the change itself.

Figure 8.2 provides an example of a definition with its history. Such a history is critical to Data Governance protocols, as it increases the trust and understanding of the information. Why a certain definition has changed can affect how we report on it or how we collect and gather its supporting data. (This aspect is also addressed by the "Audit Information, Logging, and Reporting" category within the IBM Data Governance Maturity Model, discussed in Chapter 5.) A system of record also ensures compliance with regulations such as the Sarbanes-Oxley Act and Basel II.

6.8 Integrate the Data Dictionary with the Application Environment

Business understanding is critical, yet time pressures often keep business users from leveraging available resources. For example, you might read an email or white paper and come across a term or phrase that seems ambiguous. You're not sure how it is being defined or used in your organization. You know you can find it in your company's online glossary by simply opening a web browser, but that would require you to pause in your current task. Instead, you postpone looking up the term until later. By then, you might have forgotten about it, missing some important information.

What if you could get the information immediately from where you are, without losing context? IBM InfoSphere's Business Glossary Anywhere integrates with any application on the user's desktop. So, while you are in Microsoft® Excel®, IBM Cognos®, an email application, a user manual, an online form, or anywhere else, you can simply highlight a term and right-click, and its definition will pop up instantly. In Figure 8.5, for example, the user right-clicks the business term "GL Account Number" to obtain the definition.

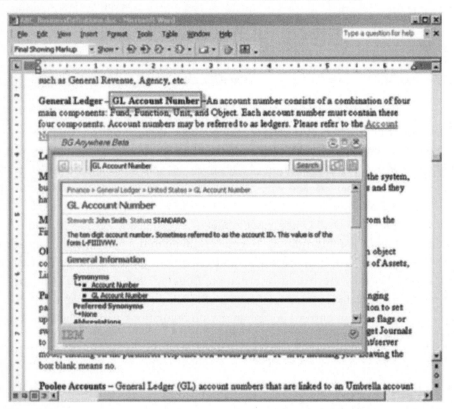

Figure 8.5: An example of using IBM InfoSphere's Business Glossary Anywhere to look up a definition within Microsoft Word.

At the end of step 6, you should have a robust data dictionary that aligns key terms across business and IT, links to technical artifacts, and integrates with the application environment.

9

Step 7:
Understand the Data

As someone once said, "You cannot govern what you do not understand." That is, before you govern data, you need to know what data you have, where it is located, and how it is related among systems. Indeed, data discovery is a crucial prerequisite to any information-centric project, such as archiving, data privacy, Master Data Management (MDM), data warehousing, data lineage, and application consolidation. For most organizations, the data discovery and analysis process is very manual, requiring months of human involvement to discover business objects, sensitive data, cross-source data relationships, and transformation logic. The result is a time-consuming and error-prone process that slows time to value.

The Data Governance organization needs to understand the data in a timely fashion, in order to drive business value from broader information-centric initiatives. Here are the sub-steps that are part of the "Understand the Data" step:

7.1 Understand each data source within the scope.

    7.1.1 Perform column- and table-level analysis.

    7.1.2 Discover legacy schemas by reverse-engineering primary-foreign key relationships.

      7.1.3 Identify the location of critical data elements inside each source.

      7.1.4 Identify the location of sensitive data inside each source.

  7.2 Understand cross-source relationships.

      7.2.1 Understand how data overlaps across data sources for critical data elements.

      7.2.2 Discover the data lineage and complex transformation logic between sources.

      7.2.3 Discover data inconsistencies and exceptions.

In the rest of this chapter, these sub-steps are described in greater detail.

7.1 Understand Each Data Source in the Scope

The initial step in the discovery process is to understand each data source included within your information-centric project.

7.1.1 Perform Column- and Table-Level Analysis

Data discovery includes column analysis and primary-foreign key analysis. Column analysis includes basic statistics about each column within a data source. IBM InfoSphere Discovery automatically generates statistics, such as implicit data type, pattern frequency, value frequency, length frequency, scale, formats, cardinality, selectivity, null count, min, max, length, and precision.

7.1.2 Discover Legacy Schemas by Reverse-Engineering Primary-Foreign Key Relationships

IBM InfoSphere Discovery is very useful when you are trying to determine the entity-relationship (ER) diagram of datasets with more than 20 tables and when data analysis is performed on poorly documented datasets. It takes all the data values in all the tables and, based on statistical analysis and patented algorithms, automatically generates an ER diagram based on an analysis of the actual data values. Figure 9.1 shows an example of this.

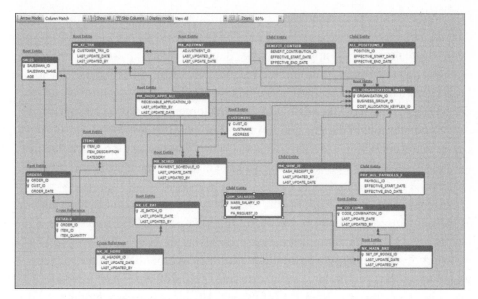

Figure 9.1: An example of IBM InfoSphere Discovery's primary-foreign key analysis.

A data analyst can review the statistics in this ER diagram for each automatically discovered key, consider alternative keys, and modify the results. IBM Info-Sphere Discovery can also discover composite keys. The ER diagram can be exported to data modeling tools such as IBM InfoSphere Data Architect or CA ERwin® Data Modeler.

Finally, IBM InfoSphere Discovery uses the primary-foreign key relationships to cluster related tables together into business entities, such as customers, orders, materials, and vendors. These business object definitions are very useful for MDM. They can also be consumed by IBM InfoSphere Optim™ to archive data, ensure data privacy, and create consistent sample sets for test data management.

7.1.3 Identify the Location of CDEs in Each Source

Critical data elements (CDEs) are those attributes that you want to include in your target schema, if you are migrating or consolidating data into a new application, MDM hub, or data warehouse. Tagging CDEs is a good starting point for constructing a unified schema across all data sources.

The Data Governance council at one company asked the data modelers to "understand all the data and to tag all the attributes." The data modelers came back in three months and said there was just too much data to accomplish the task in a meaningful period of time. The Data Governance council then asked the team to focus only on financial data. It took a year to tag 40,000 financial data attributes, with limited meaningful return to the business. The Data Governance council finally asked the data modelers to focus only on discovering sensitive data relating to their customers that would be subject to privacy regulations. This is a good example of why it is important for the Data Governance council to identify CDEs up-front. There is just too much data out there, and it is important to prioritize the efforts of the Data Governance program.

Products such as IBM InfoSphere Discovery are very helpful in this task as well, because they perform two useful functions. First, IBM InfoSphere Discovery performs an automated overlap analysis so it can quickly figure out which attributes are duplicates of other attributes in other data sources. This would have been very helpful in the example of 40,000 attributes! Second, through integration with the IBM InfoSphere Business Glossary product discussed in the previous chapter, the data analyst can tag any attribute or group of overlapping attributes with a business glossary term. This allows the business glossary terms to be connected to the actual instantiation of those terms across the data landscape. This functionality is extremely useful in establishing complete documentation that links your technical understanding of the data with the business understanding of the data.

7.1.4 Identify the Location of Sensitive Data in Each Source

Data stewards are often called upon to ensure that their data is secure and private. However, certain data fields with Personally Identifiable Information (PII) might not be subject to the required privacy safeguards. For example, a customer's Social Security number (SSN) might be residing in a field called "EMP_NUM," and the last four digits of the SSN might be part of another field called "PIN." As a result, just looking at the column headers is not sufficient.

IBM InfoSphere Discovery looks at the actual data. It can make the case that the EMP_NUM field in one table actually relates to the SSN in another table, and to the PIN column. Once gained, these physical attributes can then be linked to their corresponding business terms in the glossary.

7.2 Understand Cross-Source Relationships

Not only is it important to understand how data exists within a database, but it also is important to understand the lineage of data as it moves and is transformed from source to source. Understanding data lineage is a relatively simple task for data that is moved by a commercial ETL tool. However, what do you do when you have data moved by legacy, hand-coded programs, where the documentation is limited or non-existent?

IBM InfoSphere Discovery enables Data Governance by providing a centralized, accurate way to automatically discover, document, and understand data relationships—including transformation logic—across complex, heterogeneous data sources.

IBM InfoSphere Discovery also includes a Unified Schema Builder set of capabilities. This is a workbench for the analysis of multiple data sources and for prototyping the combination of those sources into a consolidated target like an MDM hub, a new application, or an enterprise data warehouse. The Unified Schema Builder helps build unified data-table schema prototypes, by accounting for known critical data elements and proposing statistically based matching and conflict-resolution rules before you have to write ETL code or configure an MDM hub.

7.2.1 Understand How Data Overlaps Across Data Sources for Critical Data Elements

Tagging CDEs and performing overlap analysis will help to identify the following situations:

- Data sources that contain most of the CDEs, which are a good starting point for constructing a unified schema to combine all the sources
- Data sources that are not overlapping
- Data sources that subsume other data sources
- The level of consistency between overlapping data sources

With IBM InfoSphere Discovery, overlap analysis can be executed on multiple data sources simultaneously. All columns are rapidly compared with all other columns for overlaps and then displayed in a spreadsheet format for viewing, sorting, and filtering. Figure 9.2 shows a summary of the CDEs and overlaps among three data sources (Regional_Branch, Community, and CRM).

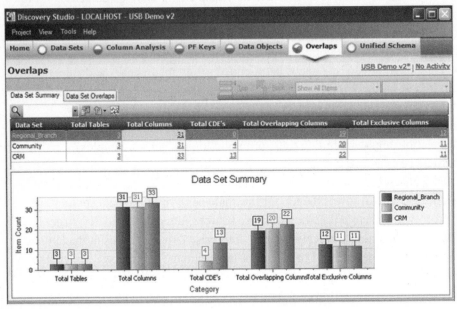

Figure 9.2: IBM InfoSphere Discovery's summary of overlaps and CDEs.

7.2.2 Discover the Data Lineage and Complex Transformation Logic Between Sources

IBM InfoSphere Discovery includes a Transformation Analyzer component that automates the discovery of complex, cross-source transformations and business rules such as substrings, concatenations, cross-references, aggregations, case statements, and arithmetic equations between two structured datasets. Figure 9.3 illustrates the steps that IBM InfoSphere Discovery follows to automatically map the columns in the Product Sales table from Application 1 to the columns in the Product Sales table in Application 2. IBM InfoSphere Discovery reads the actual data values, not just metadata such as column names, to identify these data relationships.

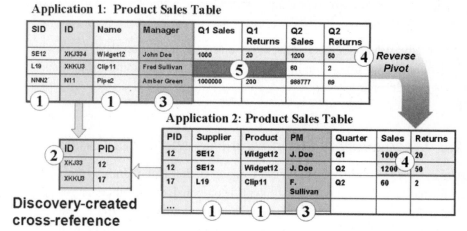

Figure 9.3: IBM InfoSphere Discovery's Transformation Analyzer component.

The numbered elements in the figure indicate the steps of the discovery process:

1. First, IBM InfoSphere Discovery discovers a matching key used to align the rows between the two datasets. In this case, the software discovers that the natural key consisting of the supplier ID and the product name relates the two tables. This key is stored in the SID and Name columns in Application 1 and in the Supplier and Product columns in Application 2. The column names "SID" and "Supplier" alone do not indicate a logical relationship, nor do "Name" and "Product." Only by reading the data values, and not the metadata, can IBM InfoSphere Discovery discern this relationship.

2. A cross-reference table is created between the primary keys in the two tables (ID in Application 1 and PID in Application 2). IBM InfoSphere Discovery uses the natural keys discovered in step 1 to cross-reference the primary keys.

3. IBM InfoSphere Discovery discovers that the PM column in Application 2 consists of the first characters of the Manager column in Application 1, followed by a period, a space, and the second token of the Manager column.

4. The values in the Q1Sales, Q1Returns, Q2Sales, and Q2Returns columns in Application 1 have been reverse-pivoted (turned into rows) in Application 2. IBM InfoSphere Discovery generates a separate mapping

for each set of pivoted columns, which create a single row (e.g., Q1Sales and Q1Returns).

5. Finally, IBM InfoSphere Discovery discovers a filter on the Q1Sales column: only rows with non-null Q1Sales have corresponding rows in Application 2.

7.2.3 Discover Data Inconsistencies and Exceptions

Because IBM InfoSphere Discovery evaluates actual data values to discover transformations, this approach also identifies inconsistencies that can result in lost revenue, customer dissatisfaction, and regulatory fines. In the real-life example in Figure 9.4, the software automatically discovers that the AGE column (which shows the age of drivers in an insurance application) is related by the case statement to the Youthful_Driver column in a second application. However, not all rows of data follow the discovered rule that the Youthful_ Driver column should be set to a "Y" when the value in the AGE column is less than or equal to 25.

Transformation
CASE WHEN AGE <=25 THEN
Youthful_Driver = 'Y' ELSE 'N' END

Hit Rate = 90%

Application A	Application B
AGE	Youthful_Driver
17	Y
24	Y
55	N
28	N
40	N
33	N
Exception¶ 83	Y
29	N
36	N
42	N

Figure 9.4: IBM InfoSphere Discovery discovers hidden relationships within insurer data.

In the example, an 83-year-old driver has a "Y" in the Youthful_Driver column. This row of data is automatically flagged as not following the discovered rule. The data steward can now research whether the driver was actually 83 years old, or if some sort of manual override caused the business rule to be violated.

10

Step 8:
Create a Metadata Repository

Metadata is "data about data." It is information regarding the characteristics of any data artifact, such as its name, location, perceived importance, quality, or value to the enterprise, and its relationships to other data artifacts that the enterprise deems worth managing. Metadata forms IT's knowledge of the business and how the information infrastructure satisfies the needs of the business. While metadata concerning a single data asset is important, it will not allow assumptions to be made regarding the data quality, currency, or integrity with respect to the entire organization. Understanding the bigger picture of how data traverses through different systems, and its usage, requires a holistic approach, typically referred to as *metadata management*.

Metadata about enterprise sources and processes can enrich their context and meaning to the point that without it these information assets can be unidentifiable, untrusted, and even unusable. How can we trust the information we see in business reports, if we do not know how it is put together? How can we identify poor data quality, if we do not have any business rules regarding quality standards? These and many more issues are the reason that proper metadata definition about information assets is critical. Whether it is source tables and columns, data models, ETL (extract, transform, and load) processes, or target systems, we need to know:

- Who created them?

- When were they created?

- What were they designed to do?

- Have they been changed?

- If they change, does the change have any effect on other information assets?

- What are their quality standards?

Here are the key sub-steps associated with creating a metadata repository:

8.1 Merge business metadata from the data dictionary and technical metadata from the discovery process.

8.2 Ensure the appropriate data lineage.

8.3 Conduct an impact analysis.

8.4 Manage operational metadata.

These sub-steps are discussed in further detail below.

8.1 Merge Business and Technical Metadata

The Data Governance program will generate a lot of business metadata from the data dictionary and technical metadata during the discovery phase. While technical metadata is critical to arm the IT staff with tools that support efficient business applications and enterprise resources, not having it linked to business metadata creates a gap between the business and technical teams. The IT staff needs to stay connected with the business, understand the business language, and support an infrastructure that is aligned with business goals.

Business and technical metadata needs to be stored in a repository such as IBM InfoSphere Metadata Workbench, so that it can be used across multiple projects. That way, when technical users are looking at tables, data transformation processes, and derivations that pull together "high value customer" data, they fully understand who those customers are, how they are defined, and what business metrics govern their status. IBM InfoSphere Metadata Workbench creates a centralized and holistic view of the entire landscape of data integration processes.

8.2 Ensure the Appropriate Data Lineage

Exposure to financial fraud is a key business driver of risk mitigation for organizations. Many of us remember the high-profile accounting scandals that eventually led the U.S. government to establish the Sarbanes-Oxley Act (SOX). The goals of SOX include the establishment and implementation of measures to enable trust in companies' accounting practices.

The demand for risk mitigation and compliance affects the way organizations manage their information. One mechanism for fraud protection, or even fraud detection, on data leveraged in financial reports is demonstrating the source of the data, where it flows, and how it is transformed as it travels through the enterprise. However, the proliferation of tools that results from traditional project-based data integration practices, or merging business units, creates a seemingly impossible exercise in navigation and integration. Making the process more transparent and efficient requires a consolidation or integration of toolsets and a metadata-driven approach to building a common foundation of answers.

Data lineage provides an audit trail for data movement through integration processes. The result of a data lineage process is the answer to basic questions such as "where did this data come from?", "where does this data go?", and "what happened to it along the way?" Figure 10.1 provides an example of a data lineage report within IBM InfoSphere Metadata Workbench. IBM InfoSphere Metadata Workbench leverages the data lineage extender to incorporate non-

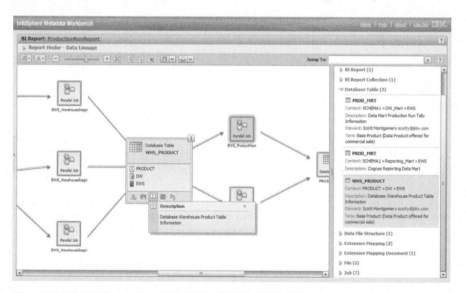

Figure 10.1: A data lineage report from IBM InfoSphere Metadata Workbench.

IBM InfoSphere data integration process, such as stored procedures, COBOL programs, and third-party ETL processes.

8.3 Conduct an Impact Analysis

The Data Governance program needs to ensure that users are able to examine all of the relationships associated with an object, thereby providing the ability to assess and mitigate risk before creating any changes. The ability to understand how a change to one data artifact affects other data artifacts is called *impact analysis*. Taking into account that changes are inevitably introduced during the development lifecycle, impact analysis allows companies to govern data more effectively.

Figure 10.2 shows a graphical dependency analysis report for a server that lists which databases, jobs, or business intelligence (BI) reports would be affected if the server had to be taken offline for maintenance. Traditionally, gathering this type of information would require navigation via multiple users and multiple toolsets, to assess the potential risk.

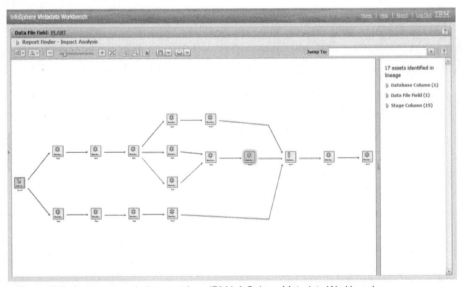

Figure 10.2: An impact analysis report from IBM InfoSphere Metadata Workbench.

8.4 Manage Operational Metadata

Operational metadata bridges the gap between what was supposed to take place and what actually took place. An enterprise may have a business intelligence environment with thousands of jobs within an ETL tool such as IBM InfoSphere DataStage, and transformations that execute in batch mode. From a Data Governance perspective, it is imperative to know in a timely manner if any jobs failed somewhere in the process, or if certain rows of data got dropped.

Some examples of operational metadata include the following:

- Whether the job run failed or had warnings

- Which database tables or files were read from, written to, or referenced

- How many rows were read, written to, or referenced

- When the job started and finished

- The stages and links that were used

- The project the job was in

- The computer that the job ran on

- Any runtime parameters that were used by the job

- The events that occurred during the job run, including the number of rows written and read on the links of the job

- The invocation ID of the job

To summarize, this chapter discusses the importance of a sound metadata strategy as a crucial underpinning of an effective Data Governance program. A metadata repository will enable data lineage, impact analysis, and the analysis of operational metadata.

11

Step 9:
Define Metrics

Data Governance tends to be centered on people and process, both of which are intangible. As a result, it is important to have an agreed-upon set of metrics, or Key Performance Indicators (KPIs), to measure and monitor the progress of the Data Governance program.

This chapter lays out the process of identifying KPIs to measure and monitor the performance of your organization's Data Governance program. It is important to recognize that these KPIs need to be tailored to the unique needs of your organization and its people, processes, and data. It is important to measure these KPIs at regular intervals and to report the results to the Data Governance council and senior executives. The business-driven and technical Data Governance KPIs need to be measured and tracked every one to three months. The Data Governance maturity assessment is of a qualitative nature and should generally be tracked on an annual basis.

IBM has developed a Data Governance scorecard within Cognos to help companies manage the performance of their Data Governance programs, discussed later in this chapter.

Here are the sub-steps that are part of the "Define Metrics" step:

9.1   Understand the overall KPIs for the business.

9.2   Define business-driven KPIs for Data Governance.

9.3   Define technical KPIs for Data Governance.

9.4   Establish a dashboard for the Data Governance maturity assessment.

Let's walk through each sub-step in greater detail.

9.1 Understand the Overall KPIs for the Business

Every business will have a hierarchy of KPIs to run its operations. IBM has published a book by Roland Mosimann, Patrick Mosimann, and Meg Dussault titled *The Performance Manager: Proven Strategies for Turning Information into Higher Business Performance* (Cognos, Inc., 2007). This book describes the hierarchy of business KPIs by job function, such as sales, marketing, finance, and risk. It is important to understand these metrics because a key objective of Data Governance is improving the trustworthiness of the data that drives these KPIs.

9.2 Define Business-Driven KPIs for Data Governance

The Data Governance program needs to define a set of focused KPIs that improve the trustworthiness of the business KPIs. For example, in a bank, the risk team will want to measure the total exposure of the bank by industry, to avoid excessive losses in case of a severe economic downturn or a specific industry trend. The bank's total exposure by industry is a business KPI. However, the bank obtains the industry data from multiple source systems and finds that the Standard Industry Classification (SIC) code is null in several cases. As a result, the industry exposure will be incorrectly calculated. The Data Governance KPI will be the percentage of customer records with null SIC codes. The Data Governance program should use this metric to track performance and to report progress to the risk team on a monthly basis.

Consider another example, from the insurance industry. From an operational perspective (and to comply with regulations such as Solvency II in Europe), a life or property-and-casualty insurer will want to limit excessive geographic risk to avoid catastrophic losses caused by such events as hurricanes or earthquakes. The insurer's total exposure by geography is a business KPI. However, the insurer finds that it has several source systems with incomplete policyholder data relating to zip or postal codes. The Data Governance KPI will be the percentage of policyholder records with null zip or postal codes. This KPI will improve the trustworthiness of the insurer's Solvency II calculations for catastrophic risk.

9.3 Define Technical KPIs for Data Governance

Technical KPIs measure progress against the technical aspects of Data Governance. Here are some examples of technical KPIs for Data Governance:

- *Metadata*—Sample KPIs include the number of data flows documented, the number of data flows monitored, the percentage of business terms with agreed-upon definitions that have been populated within the data dictionary (by domain, such as risk or finance), and the number of "orphaned assets."

  Orphans can result from importing superfluous or incomplete metadata or from deleting one or more objects in an asset's identity hierarchy. For example, if you import a database without specifying a host, the database becomes an orphaned asset in the metadata repository. Orphaned assets can be physical data resources (PDR) or business intelligence (BI) assets. PDR assets that can be orphaned include databases, data files, schemas, stored procedures, and data collections. BI assets that can be orphaned include BI collections, BI cubes, and report queries.

- *Content management*—Sample KPIs include the percentages of paper, electronic, and email documents that have been digitized and are under records management, by business unit. Additional KPIs include the percentage of core business documents, such as insurance claims or bank lending documents, which are being leveraged for content analytics; the average time (in hours) to turn around an eDiscovery request; and the percentage of unstructured metadata populated within the enterprise metadata repository.

- *Archiving*—Sample KPIs include the total storage in gigabytes, the total cost of storage, the average application-response time, and the average time in days to turn around audit queries.

- *Business Intelligence Competency Centers*—Sample KPIs include the number of users, reports, and report executions per month, by business area.

- *Security and privacy*—Sample KPIs include the number of failed audits for regulations such as Sarbanes-Oxley, the Payment Card Industry Data Security Standard, the United States Health Insurance Portability and Accountability Act, and the European Data Protection Directive.

- *Database auditing*—Sample KPIs include the number of tests conducted within the previous 12 months to test sensitive data for vulnerabilities, the number of database vulnerability exceptions discovered, the number of person hours per day spent to reconcile actual database changes against approved database change requests, the number of unauthorized changes to sensitive data, and the number of SQL errors in production databases.

9.4 Establish a Dashboard for the Data Governance Maturity Assessment

KPIs need to be developed based on a qualitative assessment of the maturity of the organization. These KPIs should generally be repeated at least once every 12 months. They measure the actual rating, the target rating, and the variance on a scale of one to five for each of the 11 categories of the IBM Data Governance Maturity Model. For reference, the eleven categories are as follows:

1. Data Risk Management and Compliance
2. Value Creation
3. Organizational Structures and Awareness
4. Policy
5. Data Stewardship
6. Data Quality Management
7. Information Lifecycle Management
8. Security and Privacy

9. Data Architecture

10. Classification and Metadata

11. Audit Information, Logging, and Reporting

Figure 11.1 shows an example of an IBM Cognos scorecard that measures the results of the Data Governance maturity assessment.

Figure 11.1: The IBM Cognos scorecard for a Data Governance maturity assessment.

In the figure, the categories of the Data Governance maturity assessment have been tweaked slightly, based on the needs of the organization. The organization selected a subset of the categories of the IBM Data Governance Maturity Model. It also added a custom category around "Information Analytics" because of the intense focus on business intelligence. In addition, it parsed the metadata into two categories: technical and business metadata. Finally, to emphasize the importance of unstructured content, the organization changed the name of the "Data Architecture" category to "Information Architecture."

12

Step 10.1:
Appoint Data Stewards

Master Data Governance is an ongoing practice whereby business leaders define the principles, policies, processes, business rules, and metrics to achieve business objectives by managing the quality of their master data. The Data Governance council marshals people, organizations, resources, priorities, and technologies to implement those declarations of policy. The Data Governance council then monitors and measures the progress toward those goals, to ensure that master data are meeting quality objectives.

The next three chapters will explore data stewardship, data quality, and Master Data Management (MDM), which are key components of Master Data Governance.

Data stewardship tends to be where the first seeds of an enterprise Data Governance program begin to germinate. Data stewardship is a quality-control discipline designed to ensure custodial care of information, to address the needs of the business. Organizations appoint data stewards who understand the business, to ensure that the information is "fit for purpose." Data stewards are not the owners of the data; rather, they are custodians responsible for improving the quality of data as an enterprise asset.

Here are the sub-steps of step 10.1; the rest of the chapter discusses these sub-steps in greater detail.

10.1.1 Appoint the chief data steward.

10.1.2 Determine the configuration of the data stewardship program (e.g., by IT system, organization, or subject area).

10.1.3 Identify executive sponsors for each data domain.

10.1.4 Recruit data stewards for each data domain.

10.1.5 Empower the Data Governance council to oversee the data stewardship program.

10.1.1 Appoint the Chief Data Steward

Data stewards should ideally report into the business. Because the data stewards will report into multiple divisions or functions, the organization should appoint a chief data steward to ensure consistency across the various stewardship roles. The chief data steward needs to be a member of the Data Governance working group and must play an active role in the overall Data Governance program.

10.1.2 Determine the Configuration of the Data Stewardship Program

There are several ways to configure a data stewardship program. These can be presented in the form of a maturity model, shown in Figure 12.1.

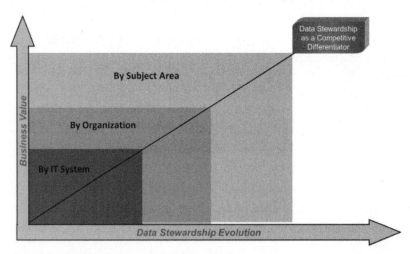

Figure 12.1: The IBM Data Stewardship Maturity Model.

Initial Maturity Level: Data Stewardship Aligned by IT System

In the most common model, data stewards are assigned to manage the data in a given IT system or application. For example, a data steward might be assigned to clean the customer data in a customer information file (CIF). In this scenario, the data steward will most likely reside within IT.

This data stewardship model is the easiest to implement because it does not require the business to have any meaningful stake in the Data Governance program. On the flip side, the IT-centric model has some drawbacks, as well. Data quality needs a business perspective to ensure that the information is fit for purpose. Because there is limited business involvement in the data stewardship program, IT will be constrained in its ability to steward data. Also, a typical organization has several CIFs or product and item hierarchies. As a result, it will be difficult, without significant manual intervention, to answer questions such as "Who are our top customers across the enterprise?" and "What are our best-selling products?"

Intermediate Maturity Level: Data Stewardship Aligned by Organization

Some enterprises will elect to deploy data stewards by job function, such as risk, marketing, and sales, or by line of business. These data stewards typically report into the business and are responsible for all the data within their respective domains. The advantage of this approach is the linkage between data stewardship and the business. A disadvantage is that the organization continues to treat enterprise data such as customer, item, vendor, and product information on a fragmented basis.

Advanced Maturity Level: Data Stewardship Aligned by Subject Area

Mature organizations will deploy a data stewardship program in conjunction with a Master Data Management program. These organizations recognize the need to have a single system of record for key master data entities, such as customer, item, vendor, and product, and will treat these data entities as an enterprise asset.

This approach allows organizations the most flexibility to address enterprise initiatives such as customer-centricity. However, this approach is also the most difficult to implement. Individual lines of business have to give up control of their data to the MDM hub.

To ensure the success of this approach, the data stewards need to be very involved in defining critical data elements, or attributes, where two or more lines of business have competing rules about how to accept adds and updates. The data steward also needs to have a clearly defined role when the business rules of two or more lines of business collide. For example, Business Line A cannot overwrite the address for a customer who also has a relationship with Business Line B. If Business Line A has an update to an address for a joint customer, it is held in a pending state. The update must be approved by Business Line B before it is accepted.

A staged approach to enterprise stewardship, with one data domain at a time, is also a best practice. As in all cases, consider your own unique situation before you design your data stewardship program.

10.1.3 Identify Executive Sponsors for Each Data Domain

The organization needs to identify executive-level sponsors for data stewardship. These sponsors will have ultimate responsibility for the data, although they will most likely delegate day-to-day activities to someone else. The selection of the executive sponsors is driven by the desired configuration of the data stewardship program.

If the data stewardship program is aligned by IT system, the executive sponsors will reside in IT and will likely be owners of specific IT systems. If the data stewardship program is aligned by organization, the executive sponsors might reside in either IT or the business or both but will in all cases be aligned by organization. Finally, if the data stewardship program is aligned by subject area, the executive sponsors will likely reside within functions such as sales, HR, finance and supply chain, depending on the associated data domains, such as customer, employee, financial data, vendor, and product.

Here are some of the responsibilities of an executive sponsor:

- Have ultimate responsibility for the quality of data within the domain

- Ensure the security and privacy of all sensitive data, such as PII and PHI, within the domain

- Appoint data stewards with day-to-day responsibility for dealing with the data quality, security, and privacy issues within the domain

- Establish and monitor metrics regarding the progress of Data Governance within the domain

- Collaborate with other executive sponsors in situations where business rules collide, to ensure that the enterprise continues to derive maximum value from its data

10.1.4 Recruit Data Stewards for Each Data Domain

As mentioned earlier, the executive data stewardship sponsors will most likely delegate the day-to-day responsibilities to someone more junior, who is able to devote sufficient time to the task. The individuals who perform these day-to-day tasks are referred to as "data stewards." Data stewards in many organizations often operate on a de facto basis. By spending significant amounts of time addressing data quality issues, they are data stewards, even if they don't know they are operating in that capacity. Sometimes business users or analysts who use or support key applications where data is created make good data stewards. For example, somebody who has worked with the underwriting or policy systems at an insurer might make a good data steward, because this individual understands the business usage of the data.

Many data stewards tend to wear multiple hats. When an organization has the right level of business sponsorship, however, there will be a natural gravitational pull to have them spend more time on their stewardship duties.

10.1.5 Empower the Data Governance Council to Oversee the Data Stewardship Program

When a data stewardship program reaches maturity, the data stewards should report into the business. At this point, it is important to ensure that there is some level of oversight across all the data stewards, to ensure a consistency in roles and responsibilities and to develop a sense of community. The Data Governance council is ideally placed to oversee the data stewardship program for consistent execution across the organization and linkage to the business. The council can enforce a sense of discipline by a consistent focus on KPIs that track the performance of the data stewardship program. The discussion on metrics in Chapter 11 covers this topic in more detail.

13

Step 10.2:
Manage Data Quality

The typical organization has lots of information about its customers, products, and vendors scattered throughout its operational systems. Without proper oversight, the quality of this data will atrophy over time. Data quality management is a discipline that includes the methods to measure, improve, and certify the quality and integrity of an organization's data. Data quality includes data standardization, matching, survivorship, and the monitoring of quality over time.

The Data Governance organization needs to establish policies to identify high-value data attributes, and the mechanism to measure the improvement of data quality over time. Here are the sub-steps associated with this "Manage Data Quality" step:

10.2.1 Establish data quality policies, including the identification of high-value data attributes.

10.2.2 Baseline data quality.

10.2.3 Build the business case.

10.2.4 Cleanse the data.

10.2.5 Monitor the data quality over time.

These sub-steps are discussed in greater detail below.

10.2.1 Establish Data Quality Policies

Every business has data that is critical to its operations. This sub-step is closely linked with step 9, on Data Governance metrics. Once the Data Governance organization has identified the business-driven Data Governance KPIs, it is easy to determine the data attributes with the highest value. For example, Standard Industry Classification (SIC) codes would be a high-value data attribute for a bank that wanted to assess its overall risk exposure by industry. Similarly, re-order levels within the materials master would be a high-value data attribute for a manufacturer looking to tightly manage its supply chain.

Additional policies are also required around the adherence to business rules. For example, a manufacturer might well determine that the re-order point cannot be null for materials where re-order planning is required.

Policies are also required around the acceptable level of data quality. For example, undeliverable mailing addresses are a key data quality issue that affects postage costs. However, the Data Governance organization might well determine that one percentage point of poor data quality is acceptable, and as long as undeliverable mailing addresses fall below that threshold, no further action is required. Finally, the Data Governance organization needs to define policies and procedures that deal with the manner in which data quality issues are addressed.

10.2.2 Baseline Data Quality

Data has to be of the appropriate quality to address the needs of the business. There are several ways to assess the quality of a dataset:

- *Validity*—The data values are in an acceptable format. For example, employee numbers have six alphanumeric characters.

- *Uniqueness*—There are no duplicate values in a data field.

- *Completeness*—There are no null values in a data field. For example, the zip or postal code should always be populated in an address table.

- *Consistency*—The data attribute is consistent with a business rule that may be based on that attribute itself, or on multiple attributes. For example, a business rule might check whether a birth year is prior to 1/1/1900 or whether the effective date of an insurance policy is prior to the birth date on the policy.

- *Timeliness*—The data attribute represents information that is not out-of-date. For example, no customer contracts have expiry dates that have passed.

- *Accuracy*—The data attribute is accurate. For example, employee job codes are accurate to ensure that an employee does not receive the wrong type of training.

- *Adherence to business rules*—The data attribute or a combination of data attributes adheres to specified business rules. (Chapter 11, on metrics, covers this topic in more detail.)

This sub-step is closely linked to the "Understand the Data" step, discussed in Chapter 9. IBM InfoSphere Information Analyzer provides an automated way to baseline the quality of data.

10.2.3 Build the Business Case

Once the Data Governance organization has identified high-value data attributes and baselined data quality, it has enough information to build a business case. Figure 13.1 lays out a hypothetical business case to improve data quality by matching duplicates within a customer database, as well as establishing whether multiple individuals are really part of the same household. The marketing

A. Total number of customers in the marketing list	950,000
B. Number of individual party matches	40,000
C. Additional duplicate individuals who are double-counted as part of a household	50,000
D. Total number of duplicate matches	90,000
E. Number of annual marketing mailings per customer	2
F. Cost per mailing	$3.25
G. Total avoidable cost of duplicate mailings (DxExF)	$585,000
H. Outbound telemarketing calls per customer per year	4
I. Cost per outbound telemarketing call	$1.50
J. Total avoidable cost of outbound telemarketing calls (DxHxI)	$540,000
K. Total avoidable cost of duplicate matches (G+J)	$1,125,000
L. Cost to implement data quality tools	$500,000
M. Annual cost of full-time customer data steward	$200,000
N. Total cost of data quality solution (L+M)	$700,000
O. Payback period	7.5 months

Figure 13.1: A hypothetical data quality business case for the marketing department.

department spends millions of dollars on mailing catalogs and making outbound telemarketing calls to customers. As a result, any reduction in the customer list by removing duplicates will flow directly to the bottom line.

Another scenario with major data quality implications is an Enterprise Resource Planning (ERP) implementation. A typical ERP implementation might involve the movement of data from dozens, if not hundreds, of legacy applications into the target system. Empirical evidence shows that more than 40 percent of the cost of an ERP project centers around data integration. In addition, data quality issues have been identified as one of the leading causes of failure of ERP projects. It is one thing to load the data correctly, and quite another to "load the correct data correctly." As a result, any ERP project needs to focus on the quality of data being migrated into the target application.

10.2.4 Cleanse the Data

IBM Initiate Master Data Service is an MDM system that includes match and link capabilities. IBM InfoSphere QualityStage helps organizations cleanse data and manage data quality. These tools facilitate the creation and maintenance of high-quality master data by matching data such as name, address, phone number, email address, and birth date.

Figure 13.2 demonstrates how a data steward can leverage a matching engine to standardize parts data. The input file contains parts data in a non-standard format, but the matching engine is able to output the data in a standardized format based on assembly instruction, quantity, type, part, size, measure, and SKU.

Input file

```
WING ASSY DRILL 4 HOLE USE 5J868A HEXBOLT 1/4 INCH
WING ASSEMBLY, USE 5J868-A HEX BOLT .25"- DRILL FOUR HOLES
USE 4 5J868A BOLTS (HEX .25) - DRILL HOLES FOR EACH ON WING ASSEM
RUDER, TAP 6 WHOLES, SECURE W/KL2301 RIVETS (10 CM)
```

Result file

Assembly Instruction	Qty	Type	Part	Size	Measure	SKU
WING DRILL	4	HOLES	HEXBOLT	.25	INCH	5J868A
WING DRILL	4	HOLES	HEXBOLT	.25	INCH	5J868A
WING DRILL	4	HOLES	HEXBOLT	.25	INCH	5J868A
RUDDER DRILL	6	HOLES	RIVET	10	CM	KL2301

Figure 13.2: A parts-standardization example (based on the white paper IBM InfoSphere Information Server: Cleansing Data and Managing Data Quality, *IBM, 2006).*

10.2.5 Monitor the Data Quality over Time

Once you have cleansed the data, you need to ensure that it remains of high quality. Too often, data is cleansed and then left on its own to get back into a low-quality state. An intensive effort is then needed to cleanse the data all over again.

The data quality process needs to consider multiple steps. Some steps are automated, and some are not. Data quality starts with improving the processes and training for data entry and inputs. You need to get those who enter the data to be consistent, and to validate the data before final submission.

We all know that the training and processes will provide, at best, only a 50 percent improvement in data quality. That is why you also need to sample and profile the data for continuous improvement. IBM InfoSphere Information Analyzer profiles data to provide a data quality assessment, analysis, and continuous monitoring, to ensure that the quality of information remains high over time.

14

Step 10.3: Implement Master Data Management

To meet fundamental strategic objectives such as revenue growth, cost reduction, and risk management, organizations need to gain control over data that is often locked within silos across the business. The most valuable of this information—the business-critical data about customers, products, materials, vendors, and accounts—is commonly known as master data. Despite its importance, master data is often replicated and scattered across business processes, systems, and applications throughout the enterprise. Organizations are now recognizing the strategic value of master data. They are developing long-term Master Data Management (MDM) action plans, to harness this information to drive corporate success.

A *master data domain* refers to a specific category of information, such as customers, products, materials, vendors, or accounts. Each data domain has specific attributes that need to be "fit for purpose." For example, a phone number is an important attribute for the customer data domain because it is important for an enterprise to have valid contact information in case of need.

There are relationships between master data domains that represent true understanding. For example, it is valuable for a bank to have a linked view of all the accounts and products for a given customer, so that it can understand the total relationship to facilitate servicing, the sale of additional products, and profitability analysis. Customers, accounts, and products represent master data domains that have a relationship.

It is useful to recognize what master data is not. Master data is not used by just one application. It is high-value data, not low-value data. Finally, it is generally not data that is updated only infrequently.

Without the proper oversight, MDM initiatives invariably result in organizational friction, because individual lines of business perceive that they have to cede control over their data to the MDM hub. We refer to this scenario as "active MDM," and that is why Master Data Governance is so critical.

Here are the sub-steps associated with implementing MDM:

10.3.1   Identify the business problem.

10.3.2   Define the subject areas of master data.

10.3.3   Identify the systems and business processes that consume the data.

10.3.4   Identify the current data sources.

10.3.5   Define the data attributes of the system of record.

10.3.6   Appoint data stewards for each system of record.

10.3.7   Establish policies for Master Data Governance.

10.3.8   Implement a data stewardship console for manual intervention and monitoring.

10.3.9   Manage potential overlay tasks.

10.3.10 Match duplicate suspects from the same source or from multiple sources to create a new master record.

10.3.11 Link related records from multiple sources.

10.3.12 Review duplications of unique identifiers.

10.3.13 Manage relationships.

10.3.14 Manage hierarchies.

10.3.15 Manage groupings.

10.3.16 Architect the Master Data Management solution.

The rest of this chapter provides more detail on each of these sub-steps.

10.3.1 Identify the Business Problem

Identifying the business problem is tied closely to the first step of the IBM Data Governance Unified Process, "Define the Business Problem." An MDM initiative needs to be sufficiently tactical to ensure a quick payback. Most MDM initiatives tend to be focused on the key objectives of growing revenues, reducing costs, and managing risk. Revenue growth might focus on customer-centricity, and cost reduction might identify vendor efficiencies, while risk management might want to improve the calculations of overall credit exposure to key counterparties.

10.3.2 Define the Subject Areas of Master Data

Although the prioritization of master data entities tends to vary by industry, there are certain common threads. Key master-data entities tend to be customer, vendor, agent, location, product, material, employee, and financial data. Customer data is, by far, the most common master data entity managed because customers are the lifeblood of any business. For most enterprises, the HR department will sponsor employee master data, and the finance department will want to ensure a consistent chart of accounts to facilitate smooth financial consolidation.

Manufacturers tend to focus on customer, vendor, product, item, and asset master data. The typical sponsors for customer data include the sales, marketing, and customer service areas. The CEO of a major industrial products company sponsored an MDM initiative when his counterpart at another company told him, "We are one of your top five customers," which is something that his own team could not easily validate. The supply chain and engineering groups have an intense interest in product and material master data, with the typical manufacturer having hundreds of thousands of SKUs across multiple hierarchies. Finally, vendor master data is of intense interest to the supply chain, procurement, and finance areas.

Insurers focus on policyholder and agent master data with business sponsors from marketing, policy administration, and distribution. Banks focus on customer, account, and product master data, sponsored by the risk management, marketing, customer service, retail banking, and corporate banking departments.

Telecommunications service providers ("telcos") have multiple systems that are geared to individual products, such as copper-based landline, wireless, and DSL. As a result, telcos need a single view of the overall relationship with their subscribers, to facilitate programs such as churn management and cross-selling additional products. Other master data entities include product, asset, customer usage, vendors, and tariffs.

Retailers tend to have an intense interest in customer, product, and vendor master data. The marketing departments at many retailers are making customer master data a cornerstone of their customer-centricity and loyalty programs. The supply chain and merchandising groups at these organizations have an intense interest in the efficient management of product master data because they already have sizeable staffs that manage hundreds of thousands of SKUs across multiple hierarchies. For example, supply chain and finance at a large retailer negotiated major discounts with their suppliers, and made effective use of manufacturer's rebates, once they understood the total spend with each vendor across all products and business units.

10.3.3 Identify the Systems and Business Processes That Consume the Data

It is important to understand which systems and business processes consume the data. The new MDM hub will also need to support those systems and business processes.

10.3.4 Identify the Current Data Sources

It is important to identify the current sources of data and the business rules associated with that data. You have probably addressed this sub-step, at least partially, earlier on in the IBM Data Governance Unified Process.

10.3.5 Define the Data Attributes of the SOR

Once again, you have probably addressed this sub-step, at least partially, earlier on in the IBM Data Governance Unified Process. It is important to agree on the data attributes of the system of record (SOR). For example, the data attributes for "customer" might include first name, last name, telephone number, Social Security number or national ID, street address, city, state, and zip or postal code. Both IBM InfoSphere MDM and IBM Initiate offer a defined data model that is useful to jumpstart an MDM implementation.

The Data Governance organization needs to act as a tie-breaker when key data attributes of the SOR are updated by more than one business process. Let's review an example from the financial services industry. A financial services company owned both a bank and a life insurance company and was in the process of implementing a centralized MDM program to better manage customer relationships.

The Data Governance team reached agreement on the 21 attributes for "customer" data. The Data Governance policy was that a customer could make a change to his or her profile by calling either the bank or the life insurance company and have those changes cascade across the entire enterprise. This process created some Data Governance issues. The bank would accept changes to date of birth with limited documentation, while the life insurance division would require supporting documentation, due to the impact on life insurance premiums. The bank believed that the life insurance process would slow them down, and the life insurance company felt that the bank's processes were too risky.

After much hand wringing and several internal meetings, the Data Governance council brokered a compromise. The customer service representatives in the bank would have a screen that flagged customers who also had a life insurance policy. If the customer did not have a life insurance policy, the bank would accept changes to the date of birth without documentation. If the bank customer also had a life insurance policy, the bank required the customer to submit supporting documentation.

10.3.6 Appoint Data Stewards for Each SOR

The organization needs to appoint data stewards for each SOR. These stewards need to reside within the business and report to the executive sponsors for their respective data domains.

The data stewards must have sufficient knowledge about the way data is being used in the enterprise's day-to-day operations. For example, the steward for customer data would reside within sales, customer service, or marketing. Similarly, the steward for product data would reside within supply chain, engineering, or research and development. Chapter 12, on data stewardship, deals with this topic in greater detail.

10.3.7 Establish Policies for Master Data Governance

The Data Governance program needs to establish policies around MDM. Examples of such policies include the following:

- Data matching rules
- Rules for automated matching versus manual intervention

- Data validation rules
- Rules that govern changes to critical data, such as a birth date in the case of a life insurer
- Naming conventions
- Identification of specific attributes as sensitive data

The implementation of these policies is addressed in the subsequent sub-steps. Please also refer to Appendix E for a sample set of Data Governance declarations.

10.3.8 Implement a Data Stewardship Console for Manual Intervention and Monitoring

Irrespective of the degree of automation in data matching, some level of manual intervention by a data steward will always be required. Both IBM InfoSphere Master Data Management Server and IBM Initiate improve the productivity of data stewards through data stewardship consoles. These consoles are called the IBM InfoSphere Master Data Management Data Stewardship User Interface (DSUI) and IBM Initiate Inspector, respectively. Figure 14.1 provides a screen shot of the DSUI. We will use the term "IBM MDM" during the remainder of this chapter to encompass IBM InfoSphere Master Data Management Server, IBM InfoSphere Master Data Management Server for Product Information Management, and IBM Initiate.

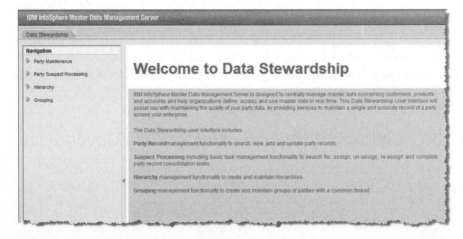

Figure 14.1: IBM InfoSphere MDM Data Stewardship User Interface, a console for data stewards.

10.3.9 Manage Potential Overlay Tasks

A potential overlay occurs when a record is updated with information that is radically different from the data already in the record. This situation is typically considered the most urgent task to resolve. For example, consider the situation illustrated in Figure 14.2. The data steward reviews a record that used to belong to Jane Lewis. However, on August 24, 2006, the record was updated. It now appears to belong to a woman named Linda Xiang. Linda Xiang and Jane Lewis are clearly not the same person, but when you look at how the record is structured, you can see that at one point Linda Xiang's data was saved over Jane Lewis' data. The cause might be a fairly common typographical data entry mistake, in which Jane Lewis' record was open on the screen when the customer service representative started typing, not realizing that he or she was typing over someone else's data.

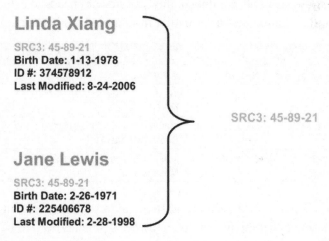

Figure 14.2: A potential overlay task.

There are also some situations in which this scenario would be perfectly valid. For instance, it is certainly plausible that a person's data would change significantly enough to flag a potential overlay task because of a marriage, divorce, move, or phone-number change. In either case, it never hurts for the data steward to investigate, double-check, and verify that users are viewing the correct person's data.

Because of their urgent nature, potential overlay tasks are generally the highest priority for the data steward to resolve. If certain data elements such as name, identity number, or phone number are completely different, IBM MDM flags these records as potential overlay tasks.

10.3.10 Match Duplicate Suspects to Create a New Master Record

Let's consider another example of how a data steward at a multi-line insurer can leverage a matching engine such as IBM Initiate Master Data Service or IBM InfoSphere Quality Stage to create a customer profile with the best data from all sources. The insurer has multiple customer information files (CIFs) within life insurance, homeowner's insurance, and auto insurance and is looking to create a customer profile with the best data from across all these lines.

As shown in Table 14.1, the insurer starts with three accounts from the life, homeowners, and auto insurance lines with similar names, but slightly different addresses and telephone numbers, and with birth dates that are either blank or inconsistent. The data steward needs to assess whether these accounts need to be linked. If these accounts are linked, the data steward needs to create a single customer profile with the best information from across the enterprise.

Table 14.1: Classic Account-to-Customer Transformation – Account View					
Source	Legacy Key	Name	Address	Phone	Birth Date
Life	70328574	John Smith Jr.	10 Main St Boston MA 02110	781-259-9945	02/05/1940
Home	80328575	Mr. John Smith	10 Main St Unit 10 Boston MA 02111	617-259-9000	
Auto	90238495	J. Smyth	Main St Bostan Mass 02110	781-295-9945	02/05/1941

Based on the similarity of the name and street addresses, the matching engine is able to determine that the life and homeowner's policies need to be linked, as shown in Table 14.2. There is still doubt about whether "J. Smyth" with the auto insurance policy is the same person as "John Smith."

Table 14.2: Customer View						
Source	Legacy Key	Name	Address	Phone	Birth Date	Cust-ID
Life	70328574	John Smith Jr.	10 Main St Boston MA 02110	781-259-9945	02/05/1940	0001
Home	80328575	Mr. John Smith	10 Main St Unit 10 Boston MA 02111	617-259-9000		0001
Auto	90238495	J. Smyth	Main St Bostan Mass 02110	781-295-9945	02/05/1941	

On further inspection, the data steward determines that the address and names are sufficiently similar that they relate to the same person. Now, how does the data steward pick from multiple, inconsistent addresses, phone numbers, and birth dates? Fortunately, that is where the rules of data survivorship come into play. The Data Governance rules of survivorship state that life insurance is the best source for birth date because that information determines premiums. Similarly, homeowner's insurance is the best source for address information because that data is directly tied to the entity being insured. On that basis, the data steward is able to assemble a customer profile using the best information from across the enterprise, as shown in Table 14.3.

Table 14.3: Customer Profile					
Source	Name	Address	Phone	Birth Date	Cust-ID
Customer Profile	Mr. John Smith Jr.	10 Main St Unit 10 Boston MA 02111	617-259-9000	02/05/1940	0001

The data stewardship console allows the steward to search for duplicate suspects based on specific criteria. The data steward determines whether the parties are a match by comparing the attributes of each suspect and then collapsing the parties based on the best attributes of each suspect. The data stewardship console then creates a new party with the consolidated attributes, and all the existing party records are rendered inactive.

10.3.11 Link Related Records from Multiple Sources

Sub-task 10.3.11 is closely related to the registry, or virtual, architectural approach to MDM discussed later. With overlays, the data steward was verifying records that already existed. With duplicate suspects, the data steward was getting rid of extra records. In this sub-task, the data steward is linking records between systems.

IBM MDM can implement registry-style Master Data Management by linking records from multiple sources that have a high likelihood of representing the same person. However, the records might not have enough data in common to be automatically linked. For example, the scenario in Figure 14.3 shows three records for "Ken Richardson," "Kenneth Richardson," and "Len K. Richardson." When you first look at these three records, they appear to be the same person. However, looking more closely at the names, you can notice some differences.

First, the first names are different: "Ken," "Kenneth," and "Len K." Second, one of the records has a user ID with a "46," while the other two records have a "64." This type of typographical transposition is very common. IBM MDM would group these records into a task, so that the data steward can verify that they are the same person, and then link them.

Ken Richardson	Kenneth Richardson	Len K Richardson
ID #: 741786649	ID #: 741786649	ID #: 741786469
DOB: 1952-4-23	DOB: 1952-4-23	DOB: 1952-4-23
SRC1: 88-88-88	SRC2: 19-26-43	SRC3: 84-34-94

Figure 14.3: Linking related records from multiple sources.

10.3.12 Review Duplications of Unique Identifiers

The need to review identifier tasks occurs when two records from the same source seem to be using the same unique identifier, such as a Social Security number, passport number, or driver's license number. Some organizations, such as those within law enforcement and Homeland Security, might consider this situation to be a high priority from a data stewardship perspective.

Figure 14.4 shows two records for people who are clearly not the same person but who have the same key identifier number. IBM MDM flags records for manual review when they contain the same unique identifier but have other attributes that reflect two different individuals.

Mia Adams-Patel	Fred Laughton
ID #: 199985648	ID #: 199985648
SRC2: 45-89-21	SRC2: 86-14-34

Figure 14.4: A review identifier task.

10.3.13 Manage Relationships

Joe and Mary each own accounts with the same bank, and they get married. By looking at their account grouping, the data steward can see that Joe has two accounts in his name (an auto loan and a credit card). Mary has three accounts in her name (a checking account, a credit card, and an auto loan). They also have three joint accounts (a mortgage loan, a checking account, and a savings account). Through the use of relationships, the data steward can develop the big picture of three account owners—Joe's accounts, Mary's accounts, and their joint accounts—to establish the credit exposure to the entire household, as shown in Figure 14.5.

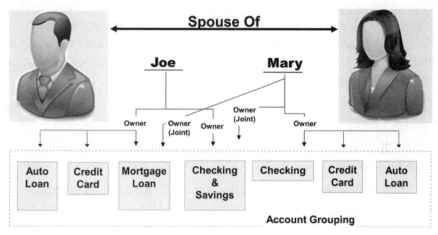

Figure 14.5: Managing relationships to determine household credit exposure.

10.3.14 Manage Hierarchies

The data stewardship console should enable a steward to add or edit a hierarchy. For example, the sales organization covering Jaguar will want to ensure that its client is eligible for the same contractual terms as Tata, which is the new parent company. As a result, the customer data steward will need to make a change to Jaguar's legal hierarchy and include it under Tata.

10.3.15 Manage Groupings

The data stewardship console should enable a steward to add or edit a grouping, or to add a party to a grouping. For example, a data steward might decide to add John Smith to the affluent market segment.

10.3.16 Architect the MDM Solution

Finally, the Data Governance organization needs to distill the requirements of the business, to determine the appropriate architecture for the MDM solution. There are multiple architectural approaches to MDM:

- *Transactional architecture*—This approach is typically built on an service-oriented architecture (SOA) foundation and is tightly integrated with existing business processes. Changes to attributes in one source system are first propagated to the centralized customer information file and then to the other source systems.

- *Registry architecture*—The data stays in place, and the MDM hub only has pointers to the source data in several systems. This approach works very well in situations such as healthcare and law enforcement, where there are specific regulations that do not permit the creation of a transactional hub.

- *Analytical architecture*—The master data is cleansed and brought into a central repository to answer questions such as "Who are our most profitable customers?" and "Who are our top vendors?" This approach does not try to change the data in the source systems; instead, it uses the MDM hub for analytical purposes only.

- *Hybrid architecture*—This approach combines various elements of the other three architectures.

IBM MDM can address all of these styles of Master Data Management.

15

Step 11:
Govern Analytics

Michael Dziekan at IBM is a long-time practitioner of Business Intelligence Competency Centers. Many of the concepts in this chapter are based on his work with IBM Cognos clients.

Many enterprises struggle with the governance of their analytic environments. Departments create their own reports with inconsistent data, and IT does not always know how data from the warehouse is being consumed and which reports are being used. Enterprises are starting to implement Business Intelligence Competency Centers (BICCs) to address these challenges.

Here are the sub-steps associated with the governance of analytics:

11.1 Define the objectives of the BICC.

11.2 Prepare the business case for the BICC.

11.3 Determine the organizational structure of the BICC.

11.4 Agree on the key functions of the BICC.

11.1 Define the Objectives of the BICC

While technology has always held the potential to transform business, its ability to do so has often been hampered by an organization's internal obstacles to adoption. Organizational complexity and the urgency of "immediate need" have resulted in stovepipe implementations of business intelligence (BI), performance management, and data warehouse solutions. This situation has resulted in fragmented skills and overall inconsistency in the management, delivery, and fulfillment of BI solutions across the enterprise.

Let's look at the example of a major bank that had big challenges in setting up its reporting environment. The end users within the bank had cobbled together thousands of Microsoft Access® databases because the enterprise data warehouse was perceived to be overly inflexible and expensive, and it took too long to produce new reports. The Data Governance organization commissioned a BICC to focus on end-user education and to reduce the cost and turnaround times to produce new reports.

As BI becomes increasingly more strategic, organizations are responding by creating working teams of IT and BI users, now commonly known as BICCs. A BICC is an organizational structure that groups people with interrelated disciplines, domains of knowledge, experience, and skills, for the purpose of promoting expertise throughout an organization. A BICC is also known as a Center of Excellence (COE), Competency Center, or Center of Knowledge.

A BICC can help in the following different ways:

- Deliver BI capabilities through a consistent set of skills, standards, and best practices.

- Enable repeatable and successful BI deployment through the development and focus on people, technology, and process, in ways that make sense to an entire organization or division, rather than just a single project.

If BI is to extend beyond tactical deployments to become a broad-based solution, a managed and predictable approach is needed. A BICC is essential to the strategic deployment of BI. It increases the probability of success at a lower cost in the following ways:

- Driving end-user adoption and eliminating the gap between business and IT

- Consolidating best-practice functions and services, allowing rapid and repeatable successes from other deployments

- Centralizing competency and operational efficiency, which maximizes the use of technology resources and assets

- Ensuring higher and faster adoption of the complete BI lifecycle and "single version of the truth" across the entire enterprise, which improves user satisfaction and self-service

- Enforcing a BI standard through registration, guidance, and the ability to identify new opportunities to leverage BI, resulting in an alignment of technology to strategic goals and a clarity of vision for future coordinated BI

- Educating key stakeholders about the advantages of employing BI

11.2 Prepare the Business Case for the BICC

Return on investment (ROI) is critical to gain buy-in from senior management. The BICC might require some upfront investment in people and technology, so it is important to establish a "hard dollar" ROI early in the process.

Typically, a BICC will result in IT efficiencies by centralizing infrastructure such as servers and by standardizing business intelligence, performance management, analytics, and data management tools and processes. Business users will often subscribe to the BICC's services, with potentially significant cost savings compared with separate, siloed implementations. Shared service centers should also provide a central pool of talent to educate and support the business users. This process will drive increased end-user adoption and higher levels of self-service by the business. By creating a common location for the BICC functions, IT leverages economies of scale with common education and support programs.

11.3 Determine the Organizational Structure of the BICC

The BICC structure varies depending on the needs of the organization and its level of maturity, as shown in Figure 15.1. The BICC may be an IT-only initiative, designed to focus on consolidating the system knowledge necessary to ensure a consistent enterprise strategy for BI. Alternatively, the BICC may be organized by lines of business, to focus on the functional business skills and capabilities sponsored by business executives. Some BICCs are centralized at a corporate head-office level, while others are loose networks of regional, divisional, and functional teams made up of business and IT personnel.

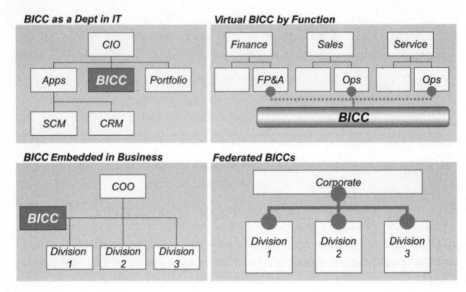

Figure 15.1: BICC organizational structures.

The design of the BICC can be centralized or decentralized, based on full-time employees or a virtual set of community skills. Its organization depends on the functions for which it is responsible and the problems that it is seeking to resolve.

11.4 Agree on the Key Functions of the BICC

Figure 15.2 portrays the typical functions of a BICC:

- *Advice and consultancy*—The BICC provides a functional area of the business with advice, guidance, mentoring, and internal consulting, so that the project teams can become self-sufficient with respect to their BI needs.

- *Community services*—The BICC is responsible for designing and building BI content, such as common reports and data packages, for use by the broader business communities.

- *Communication and evangelism*—The BICC communicates and promotes the status, progress, accomplishments, and successes of the BI program to facilitate cultural change.

- *Enterprise technical architecture*—The BICC builds and supports the technical infrastructure that supports the BI needs of the business.

- *Support*—The BICC provides a BI help-desk function to the business.

- *Education*—The BICC trains and educates business users on various BI technologies.

- *IT governance alignment*—The BICC aligns with broader IT Governance processes and steering committees, such as project and change management, portfolio management, vendor management, and license management.

- *Data Governance alignment*—The BICC interfaces with existing Data Governance programs across the organization. It tends to be at the receiving end of the "information supply chain" and needs trusted data. For example, the CEO of a major insurance company commissioned a new Data Governance program when he found that reports from different parts of his organization contained inconsistent data. In another situation, the BICC department within a government agency found that its downstream analysts could not trust the data coming out of their SAP financials and accounting systems, although the IT owners of those systems felt that the quality of data was "just fine."

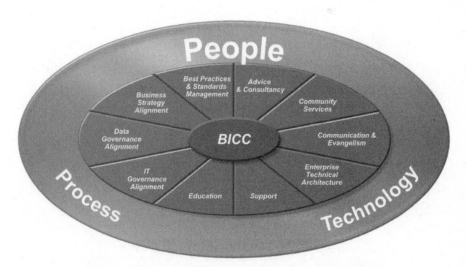

Based on IBM research with over 300 Cognos customers with Competency Centers - global across multiple sizes of organization and multiple industries

Figure 15.2: The typical functions of a BICC.

- *Business strategy alignment*—The BICC aligns with corporate business strategy to ensure that technology-related initiatives are meeting the most important needs and priorities of the business.

- *Best practices and standards management*—The BICC provides a clear process and repository for approving and sharing BI best practices and standards across the enterprise.

16

Step 12:
Manage Security and Privacy

This chapter describes the policies, practices, and controls used by an organization to mitigate risk and protect data assets and includes content from the IBM InfoSphere Guardium marketing team.

In an increasing number of enterprises, the Data Governance organization is charged with setting security and privacy strategy, in conjunction with the chief information security officer (CISO). There are several drivers for Data Governance security and privacy. The leading business driver for building a comprehensive program in this category has been to meet costly regulatory requirements. Regulatory requirements can be specific to an industry, or they can cut across industry boundary lines to affect a wide range of business sectors. One of those wide-ranging regulatory requirements in the United States is the Sarbanes-Oxley Act. This act has provisions for executive management to put controls around financial data for the highest level of integrity.

Here are the sub-steps associated with managing security and privacy:

12.1   Align with key stakeholders.

12.2   Gather the enterprise security architecture blueprint.

12.3   Tighten database change controls.

12.4   Automate the compliance workflow process.

12.5   Define sensitive data.

12.6   Discover sensitive data.

12.7   Classify and tag sensitive data.

12.8   Encrypt sensitive data.

12.9   Protect sensitive data within non-production environments.

12.10   Monitor applications for fraud.

12.11   Prevent cyber-attacks.

12.12   Redact sensitive information within unstructured documents.

The rest of this chapter reviews these sub-steps in greater detail.

12.1 Align with Key Stakeholders

This sub-step is closely related to the second step of the IBM Data Governance Unified Process, "Obtain Executive Sponsorship." Here are the key stakeholders associated with an effective Data Governance program focused on security and privacy:

- *The CISO* is an important sponsor who sets the overall policy for security and privacy across the organization.

- *The chief risk officer* might not necessarily be a part of the security organization or the IT establishment, but instead might have a reporting chain into the chief financial officer. Because compliance programs tend to be the leading driver for data security and privacy projects, the Data Governance program can establish value with the chief risk officer by improving the accuracy and lowering the cost of compliance reports.

- *Enterprise architecture* includes the chief architect, or someone who works for the chief architect, such as an enterprise security IT architect. As business owners deploy applications, the security IT architect plays a key role in establishing how the Data Governance security and privacy program is designed, deployed, and enforced within the overall architecture of the enterprise. Security IT architects rely on functional and non-functional requirements to establish blueprints and "guidepost" standards to be followed by the application developers.

- *Business sponsorship,* or the lack thereof, has plagued many security programs for years. Many business executives view information security organizations negatively, until an unfortunate incident such as a "data breach" forces radical, rapid, and costly changes. The Data Governance security and privacy program should partner with the business to lower the costs associated with regulatory requirements. The maturity of the Data Governance security and privacy program may also be assessed based on the ability to react to dynamic business conditions, while maintaining a flat cost curve.

When developing and implementing appropriate security and privacy policies, the Data Governance team needs to balance the interests of the security and risk organizations for more restrictive information access with the needs of the business for easier information access. An extreme example would be a system that is completely locked down. Obviously, the system would be highly secure, but it would not address the needs of the business.

12.2 Gather the Enterprise Security and Privacy Architecture Blueprint

The next step is to inventory all the relevant security controls and establish a security blueprint architecture. The security blueprint architecture should be used as a reference artifact for both enterprise IT and the business. There are many aspects to a security blueprint architecture, similar to building a house and determining the number and location of its rooms. However, you should focus on just those key areas that matter most to the maturity of your program. This chapter focuses on the data-centric aspects of security and privacy.

12.3 Tighten Database Change Controls

According to the white paper *Data Security, Governance, and Privacy: Protecting the Core of Your Business*, by Ron Ben-Natan (Guardium, 2006), most organizations have formal policies that govern how and when privileged users such as database administrators, help desk members, and outsourced personnel can access database systems. However, organizations do not always have effective mechanisms to monitor, control, and audit the actions of these privileged users. To make matters worse, accountability is difficult to achieve because privileged users often share the credentials used to access database systems.

Monitoring privileged users helps ensure Data Governance in the following ways:

- *Data privacy*—Monitoring ensures that only authorized applications and users are viewing sensitive data.

- *Database change control*—Monitoring ensures that critical database structures and values are not being changed outside of corporate change control procedures.

- *Protection against external attacks*—A successful, targeted attack frequently results in the attacker gaining privileged user access. For example, an outsider in Uzbekistan might look like an insider because he has authenticated access, until you look at other identifying information such as the user's location.

An organization will want to track all database changes to the following:

- *Database structures* such as tables, triggers, and stored procedures. For example, the organization will want to detect accidental deletions or insertions in critical tables that affect the quality of business decisions.

- *Critical data values* such as data that affects the integrity of financial transactions.

- *Security and access control objects* such as users, roles, and permissions. For example, an outsourced contractor might create a new user account with unfettered access to critical databases and then delete the entire account, eliminating all traces of her activity.

- *Database configuration files* and other external objects, such as environment/registry variables, configuration files (e.g., NAMES.ORA), shell scripts, OS files, and executables such as Java™ programs.

IBM InfoSphere Guardium Database Activity Monitor offers a solution that creates a continuous, fine-grained audit trail of all database activities, including the "who," "what," "when," "where," and "how" of each transaction. This audit trail is continuously analyzed and filtered in real-time, to identify unauthorized or suspicious activities. To enforce separation of duties, all audit data is stored in a secure, tamper-proof repository external to monitored databases.

IBM InfoSphere Guardium Database Activity Monitor's solution has a minimal impact on database performance and does not require any changes to databases or applications. IBM InfoSphere Guardium Database Activity Monitor also enables an organization to automate the time-consuming process of tracking all observed database changes and reconciling them with authorized work orders within existing change-ticketing systems, such as BMC Remedy and custom change management applications. For example, a large financial institution set up an automated change-reconciliation process with IBM InfoSphere Guardium Database Activity Monitor. Figure 16.1 shows a sample of the results. Previously, the institution's DBAs were spending more than an hour each day manually reconciling actual database changes with approved change ticket requests, using spreadsheets.

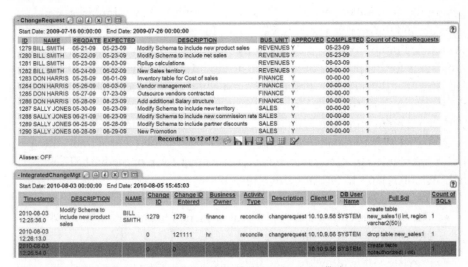

Figure 16.1: IBM InfoSphere Guardium provides change auto-reconciliation.

12.4 Automate the Compliance Workflow Process

Some organizations believe that reviewing their logs from time to time will be sufficient to pass their audits. Auditors, however, want to know three things that cannot be fully addressed by logging solutions:

- You are actually protecting your data.

- You monitor database access and can prove compliance.

- You have implemented a formal oversight process.

IBM InfoSphere Guardium automatically generates compliance reports on a scheduled basis and distributes them to stakeholders for electronic approval. These reports, including escalation and sign-off reports, enable organizations to demonstrate the existence of an oversight process for audit purposes.

12.5 Define Sensitive Data

Governments are mandating controls around personally identifiable information (PII) that, if ignored, could lead to identity fraud and a lack of trust in government or business-issued credentials. The European Union has established the Personal Data Protection Directive as the framework for privacy protection governing its member countries. Many other countries have similar regulations around the world. The U.S. Congress, for example, has enacted the Health Insurance Portability and Accountability Act of 1996 (HIPAA), which includes provisions for the privacy of protected health information (PHI). In addition, industry coalitions are developing sector-specific governance standards, such as the Payment Card Industry Data Security Standard (PCI DSS).

According to guidance from the Centers for Disease Control and Prevention (CDC), PHI is individually identifiable health information that is transmitted by, or maintained in, electronic media or any other form or medium. This information relates to one or more of the following:

- The past, present, or future physical or mental health or condition of an individual

- Provision of health care to an individual

- Payment for the provision of health care to an individual

If the information identifies (or provides a reasonable basis to believe it can be used to identify) an individual, it is considered PHI.

The Payment Card Industry Security Standards Council has defined PCI DSS for the protection of sensitive cardholder information. PCI DSS applies to all financial institutions, merchants, and service providers that store, transmit, or process cardholder data. According to the PCI DSS, sensitive cardholder data includes the following types of information:

- Primary account number (PAN)

- Cardholder name

- Service code, a three- or four-digit number on the magnetic stripe that specifies acceptance requirements and limitations for a magnetic-stripe-read transaction

- Expiration date

- Full magnetic stripe data

- Card validation value or code, the three-digit value (or four-digit value, in the case of American Express) printed on the card that ties each piece of plastic to the credit card account number

- PIN and PIN block

The cardholder name and service code are considered sensitive data for the purposes of PCI DSS only when they are stored in conjunction with the PAN. Organizations need to have Data Governance policies to discover sensitive cardholder data and to mask this data to prevent unauthorized usage.

Finally, proprietary data should also be considered sensitive. For example, the recipes for food products, internal financial reports, and the intellectual property for manufacturing processes should be considered sensitive data because they are critical to the ultimate business success of the organization.

12.6 Discover Sensitive Data

This sub-step, based on content from IBM InfoSphere Optim white papers, is closely associated with step 7, "Understand the Data." Some sensitive data is easy to find. For instance, credit card numbers in a column named "credit_card_ num" will be simple to recognize. Most application databases, though, are more complex. Sensitive data is sometimes compounded with other data elements or buried in text or comment fields. Subject matter experts can sometimes offer insight, but only if they fully understand the system.

Figure 16.2 illustrates an example. Table A contains telephone numbers in the "PHONE" column. However, in Table B, the telephone number is obscured within a compound field made up of time, phone number, and date, in the "TRANSACTION_NUMBER" column. Both instances represent confidential information that must be protected. While data analysts can clearly recognize the telephone number in Table A, they might well overlook it in Table B. Every missed occurrence of private information represents a risk to the organization.

TABLE A		
DATE	PHONE	TIME
10-28-2008	555 908 1212	13:52:49

TABLE B
TRANSACTION_NUMBER
1352555908121210282008

Figure 16.2: Confidential information hidden in compound fields poses a privacy risk for the organization.

IBM InfoSphere Discovery enables organizations to identify instances of confidential data across the environment, whether that data is clearly visible or is obscured from view. IBM InfoSphere Discovery works by examining data values across multiple sources, to determine the complex rules and transformations that may hide sensitive content. It can locate confidential data items contained within larger fields, as described in the example, or separated across multiple columns.

12.7 Classify and Tag Sensitive Data

Once you have discovered sensitive data, you must tag it with metadata classifications such as "Privacy-Restricted" or "Regulated Record." This approach enables organizations to implement consistent access policies and audit processes across items with similar properties. IBM InfoSphere Guardium automatically assigns customizable, granular access policies to groups of objects, to regulate who has access to them, from which applications and locations, at what times, using which SQL commands, and so on.

12.8 Encrypt Sensitive Data

Encryption is used to render sensitive data unreadable, so that an attacker cannot gain unauthorized access to data. The Data Governance organization needs to work closely with the CISO to address both encryption of data-in-transit as well as data-at-rest. Encryption of data-in-transit ensures that an attacker cannot eavesdrop at the networking layer and gain access to the data when it is sent to the database client. Encryption of data-at-rest ensures that an attacker cannot extract the data, even by stealing the actual storage media on which the databases are contained, such as server hard drives and backup tapes.

12.9 Protect Sensitive Data Within Non-Production Environments

Sensitive data embedded within test and training environments represents a potential exposure for organizations. Commonly, live production systems, which can include confidential data, are cloned to a test, or training, environment. Developers and quality assurance testers find it easy to work with live data because it produces test results that everyone can understand. But do non-production environments actually require live data? The answer is "no." Using realistic data is essential to testing, but live data values are not specifically necessary. Capabilities for de-identifying or masking production data offer a best-practice approach to protect sensitive data while supporting the testing process.

Data masking is the process of systematically transforming confidential data elements such as trade secrets and PII into realistic, but fictionalized, values. Data masking represents a simple concept, but it is technically challenging to execute. Finding and masking data is part of the solution. However, there is an added complication. You need the capability to propagate masked data elements to all related tables in the database, and across databases, to maintain referential integrity. For example, suppose a masked data element, such as a telephone number, is a primary or foreign key in a database table relationship. This masked data value must be propagated to all related tables in the database, or across data sources. If the data is a portion of another row's data, it must be updated with the same data as well.

IBM InfoSphere Optim Data Privacy Solution can apply a variety of proven data transformation techniques to mask sensitive, real data with contextually accurate, realistic data. Users can mask data in a single database, or across multiple related systems. These capabilities make it easy to de-identify many types of sensitive information, such as birth dates, bank account numbers, street addresses, and national identifiers such as Canada's Social Insurance numbers or Italy's Codice Fiscale. Figure 16.3 offers an example of the data-masking capabilities of IBM InfoSphere Optim Data Privacy Solution.

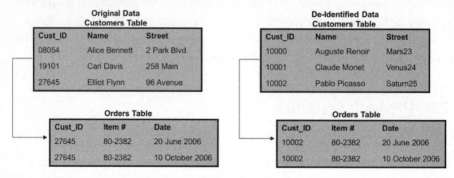

Figure 16.3: Data masking with IBM InfoSphere Optim Data Privacy Solution.

12.10 Monitor Applications for Fraud

Multi-tier enterprise applications such as Oracle and SAP, and even those that rely on an application server such as IBM WebSphere, mask the identity of end-users at the database connection level by using an optimization mechanism known as *connection pooling*. Using pooled connections, the application aggregates all user traffic within a few database connections that are identified only by a generic service account name. As a result, organizations find it challenging to associate specific database transactions with particular application end-users.

The primary purpose of application-layer monitoring is to detect fraud and other abuses of legitimate access that occur via enterprise applications, rather than via direct access to the database. IBM InfoSphere Guardium Database Activity Monitor resolves application user IDs by observing all interactions between applications and database servers, at the network and OS level, from outside the database.

12.11 Prevent Cyber-Attacks

Perimeter defenses, such as firewalls and anti-virus systems, are no longer sufficient to protect against motivated cyber-criminals, who use sophisticated techniques to penetrate back-end databases.

SQL injection is an example of a code-injection technique used by hackers to exploit Web application vulnerabilities. An organization needs to create and enforce real-time, proactive policies in the following areas (see Appendix E for a sample set of Data Governance declarations):

- *Access policies* identify anomalous behavior, by continuously comparing all database activity to a baseline of normal behavior. For example, SQL injection attacks typically exhibit patterns of database access that are uncharacteristic of standard applications, such as the creation of new tables by hackers into which they store stolen data or malware.

- *Exception policies* are based on definable thresholds, such as an excessive number of failed logins or SQL errors. SQL errors can indicate that an attacker is "looking around" for names of key tables by experimenting with SQL commands using different arguments (such as "Credit_Card_Num" or "CC_Num"). Exception policies can also be based on specific SQL error codes from the database, such as "ORA-00903: Invalid table name" or "ORA-00942: Table or view does not exist." Such error codes may indicate hacking behavior.

- *Extrusion policies* examine data leaving the database for specific data value patterns, such as credit card numbers, or a high volume of returned records that might indicate a breach.

- *Pre-configured policy signatures* identify attempts to exploit unpatched vulnerabilities or system functions (e.g., system stored procedures with known vulnerabilities or default system accounts that have not been disabled).

IBM InfoSphere Guardium Database Activity Monitor provides responses to policy violations that are fully customizable and can include the following:

- SNMP and SMTP real-time alerts

- Automated terminations, such as account logouts from the database system or VPN connection shut-downs

- Blocking, via host-based agents, that immediately terminates sessions when policies are violated (such as outsourced DBAs attempting to view or change sensitive tables)

- Forwarding of policy violations to enterprise-wide Security Information and Event Management (SIEM) systems, such as IBM Tivoli SIEM

Finally, IBM InfoSphere Optim pureQuery identifies SQL injection threats at design time, to ensure that they never get into production.

12.12 Redact Sensitive Information Within Unstructured Documents

According to the white paper *IBM Optim Data Redaction: Reconciling Openness with Privacy* (Joshua Fox and Michael Pelts, IBM, 2010), redaction is the process of removing sensitive content from an information source. Redaction is usually accomplished through the liberal use of black marking pens or whiteout fluid for paper documents and the electronic equivalent for digital documents. Many types of documents require redaction, including tax liens, property deeds, birth certificates, healthcare discharge summaries, and patient histories.

The Data Governance organization needs to balance the dual objectives of openness and privacy when dealing with redaction solutions. For example, regulations generally specify that only people with a valid business purpose may see certain entities. Thus, a physician might see a patient's medical information, but not sensitive financial information, while the reverse is true for a billing clerk. Similarly, for eDiscovery, the United States Federal Rules of Civil Procedure specify that the litigant's attorney can see privileged client-attorney information, while the opposing counsel may not; the judge, in some cases, can see all forms of information.

IBM InfoSphere Optim Data Redaction uses test extraction techniques to implement redaction policies that have been established by the Data Governance program.

17

Step 13:
Govern Lifecycle of Information

Information Lifecycle Governance refers to a systematic, policy-based approach to information architecture, classification, collection, use, archival, retention, and deletion. Because Information Lifecycle Governance is a specialized competency area, this chapter is meant to provide only a brief overview to Data Governance practitioners.

IBM Information Lifecycle Governance is a comprehensive compliance platform that enables organizations to control and manage the lifespan of their information. From a Data Governance perspective, it helps organizations address the following challenges, which are depicted in Figure 17.1:

- *Content assessment*—Address unmanaged "content in the wild," which helps to assess and decide what information to manage, trust, and leverage.

- *Content collection and archiving*—Manage the explosion of information volumes and types.

- *Advanced classification*—Reduce the burden on end users and improve the ability to classify information.

- *Records management*—Enforce retention and disposition policies, and confidently dispose of information.

- *eDiscovery search and analytics*—Respond to eDiscovery, audit, and internal investigation requests quickly and cost-effectively.

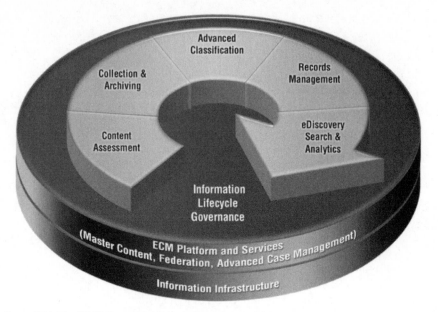

Figure 17.1: The IBM Information Lifecycle Governance model.

Here are the sub-steps associated with governing the lifecycle of information:

13.1 Establish an information architecture.

13.2 Baseline database sizes and storage architecture.

13.3 Discover business objects.

13.4 Classify data and define service levels.

13.5 Archive data and unstructured content.

13.6 Establish policies for managing test data.

13.7 Define policies for the legal discovery of electronic documents.

13.8 Analyze content.

The sub-steps are described in greater detail below.

13.1 Establish an Information Architecture

The Data Governance team needs to ensure that the organization sets standards for information architecture. More importantly, the Data Governance council needs to have the authority to enforce architectural standards. Information architecture has an important role in driving overall IT efficiency. For example, the standardization of tools and retirement of legacy applications is critical as organizations look to reduce license, software maintenance, and support costs. Standard naming conventions are also important, for things such as lab testing codes across hospitals and clinics within a county-wide healthcare system.

13.2 Baseline Database Sizes and Storage Architecture

Gaining a complete understanding of which areas are accumulating the most information allows an organization to apply the most effective Information Lifecycle Governance strategy. The source of the following information is an IBM white paper, *Control Application Data Growth Before It Controls Your Business* (September 2009).

Data duplication has significantly contributed to growth statistics. Organizations frequently clone or copy production databases to support other functions, or for application development and testing. They also maintain several backup copies of critical data, or implement mirrored databases to protect against data loss. Finally, disaster recovery plans require data duplication, to store critical data in an alternate location.

All of this duplication has created what is known as the "data multiplier effect." As data is duplicated, storage and maintenance costs increase proportionally. Figure 17.2 provides an example of a production database that

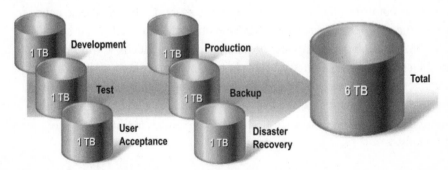

Figure 17.2: The actual data burden equals the size of the production database plus all replicated clones.

contains one terabyte of data. When that database is copied for backup, disaster recovery, development, testing, and user acceptance, the total data burden increases from one terabyte to six terabytes.

13.3 Discover Business Objects

You cannot govern data if you do not understand it, so it is critical that you first document your existing data landscape, using data discovery. Data discovery analyzes data values and patterns to identify the relationships that link disparate data elements into logical units of information, or *business objects*, such as customer, patient, or invoice.

These business objects provide essential input for archiving. Without an automated process to identify data relationships and define business objects, organizations can spend months performing manual analysis, with no assurance of completeness or accuracy. IBM InfoSphere Discovery automatically identifies relationships and defines business objects. It is covered in further detail in Chapter 9, "Understand the Data."

13.4 Classify Data and Define Service Levels

The amount of unstructured content in a typical enterprise is growing at an astonishing rate every year. From a Data Governance perspective, it is important to catalog this vast quantity of information so that it can be effectively managed by a content management system. Legal discovery is a good business example of the importance of document and email classification.

Consider an enterprise that is targeted for a lawsuit. It needs to ensure that potentially relevant documents and emails are automatically classified and placed under the control of the records management system. The enterprise needs to assign the appropriate retention and disposition rules to each document. To control storage and legal review costs, the enterprise needs to filter out irrelevant data such as company bulletins, newsletters, personal email, and personal documents that have no relevance to the pending legal case. The records-management team starts with a list of keywords provided by the legal team and fine-tunes the keywords over time to ensure that the classification system works optimally.

IBM InfoSphere Classification Module allows enterprises to create new taxonomies or add content to existing taxonomies, by analyzing the full text of documents and emails.

13.5 Archive Data and Unstructured Content

Let's consider an example from the telecommunications industry. The typical large telco generates enormous amounts of data on a regular basis. For example, a telco will generate billions of call detail records (CDRs) annually, which need to be stored and analyzed. CDR storage becomes cumbersome and expensive over time. One large telco found that it had nearly four terabytes of CDR data, which had almost doubled over the previous two years. The telco had multiple versions of CDR data in the archive, in the data warehouse, and for analytics. The billing application had 12 database clones. There were additional copies for disaster recovery. The telco even found that it had vintage tape drives with data it never knew existed.

The Data Governance program was engaged to set up a policy around archiving, retention, and deletion, with the objective of reducing storage costs without adversely affecting the business. Some of the policy questions included "How many months of CDR data do we need to maintain in the warehouse?" and "For data older than three months, can we just keep summary data in the warehouse?"

From a Data Governance perspective, an organization needs to archive both structured and unstructured content to reduce storage costs, improve system performance, and ensure compliance with regulatory requirements. In particular, unstructured content in the form of emails and other documents makes up more than 80 percent of the content within a typical enterprise. Indeed, some organizations have already recognized this paradigm shift and have rebranded their programs as "Information Governance." This content needs to be archived to reduce storage costs.

IBM InfoSphere Content Collector is an archiving solution designed to archive content within Lotus® Domino®, Microsoft Exchange, Microsoft SharePoint®, and Windows® file systems. In addition, IBM InfoSphere Content Collector allows content to be dynamically declared as a record using IBM InfoSphere Enterprise Records. Finally, it leverages the metadata from IBM InfoSphere Classification Module to make on-the-fly classification decisions.

Storing archived data according to its business value is a logical component of an integrated data management strategy. A three-tier classification strategy is a useful way to approach the problem. Current transactions are maintained in high-speed, primary storage. Reporting data are relocated to mid-tier storage. Reference data are retained on a secure Write Once, Read Many (WORM) device, keeping it available in case an audit request should arise. This approach to a tiered storage and archiving strategy is a good way to reduce costs and maximize business value. IBM InfoSphere Optim Data Growth provides proven database archiving capabilities, empowering organizations to segregate historical data from current data and to store it securely and cost-effectively, while maintaining universal access.

13.6 Establish Policies for Managing Test Data

According to the white paper *Enterprise Strategies to Improve Application Testing* (IBM, April 2008), it is typically impractical to clone an entire production database, made up of hundreds of interrelated tables, just for testing purposes. First, there is a capacity, cost, and time issue with provisioning an entirely new database environment just for testing. Second, there is a quality issue: when working with large test databases, developers might find it difficult to track and validate specific test cases.

Here are some of the requirements for effective test data management:

- *Create realistic data.* It is important to create a smaller, realistic subset of data that accurately reflects application production data.

- *Preserve the referential integrity of the test data.* The data subsets need to respect the referential integrity rules enforced within the database and the applications. Typically, application-enforced referential integrity is more complex. For example, the application may include relationships that use compatible but not identical data types, composite and partial columns, and data-driven relationships.

- *Force error and boundary conditions.* Creating realistic subsets of related test data from a production database is a reasonable start. However, it is sometimes necessary to edit the data to force specific error conditions, or to validate specific processing functions.

- *Mask and transform test data.* With the increased focus on data privacy, the ability to transform and de-identify sensitive data in the development and testing environments is critical to prevent data breaches and severe penalties.

- *Compare before and after test data.* The ability to compare test data before and after successive tests is essential to the overall quality of the application. This process involves the comparison of each test iteration against baseline test data to identify problems that otherwise could go undetected—especially when tests potentially affect hundreds or thousands of tables.

IBM InfoSphere Optim Test Data Management Solution streamlines the creation and management of test environments, subsets and migrates data to build realistic and right-sized test databases, masks sensitive data, automates test result comparisons, and eliminates the expense and effort of maintaining multiple database clones.

13.7 Define Policies for the Legal Discovery of Electronic Documents

Discovery or settlement? That is the question corporate counsels around the world are asking, especially if they are involved in litigation within the U.S. federal court system and the amended Federal Rules of Civil Procedure (FRCP). The volume of electronically stored information (ESI) subject to electronic discovery (eDiscovery) demands is typically so huge that it is often less costly to settle a suit than to undertake the extensive discovery process necessary to litigate it. In fact, the internal IT and external costs of defending a lawsuit can exceed $1 million for some companies. The cost of non-compliance with FRCP-driven requirements can easily be higher, due to sanctions, fines, and damage to the corporate reputation. Organizations need automated tools to gain access and early insight into case-related content, and to formulate their eDiscovery plans within their meet-and-confer schedules.

IBM InfoSphere eDiscovery Manager and IBM InfoSphere eDiscovery Analyzer can reduce eDiscovery costs. For example, when a discovery request comes in, an organization can use IBM InfoSphere eDiscovery Manager to collect potentially relevant ESI by performing keyword or date-range searches.

This step alone might identify 100,000 potentially relevant pieces of content in an archive containing two million items.

Going a step further, IBM InfoSphere eDiscovery Analyzer can quickly identify and flag nonresponsive content, potentially reducing the possible case-relevant content pool by another ten to fifteen percent. Because the going rate for outside analysis is approximately $1 per email, and because many organizations are managing hundreds of active cases, the ability to sift quickly through "noise" can help an organization dramatically reduce eDiscovery review costs.

13.8 Analyze Content

Content analytics is an emerging field of analytics that enables companies to unlock the insights contained in unstructured content. This unstructured content can include forms, documents, comment fields in databases, web pages, customer correspondence, and other information that is not stored within structured data fields. Content analytics offers the ability to access, sort, and analyze content, and then combine it with structured data and other existing information resources and applications, for reporting and analytics.

Content analytics is a natural extension of business intelligence. Many organizations already use business intelligence for "data-driven decision-making." This decision-making process is based on insights gleaned from records of past transactions and other structured information typically housed in data warehouses. Organizations can supplement these business intelligence methods with content techniques, which can be used to expose trends within unstructured content. For example, organizations can analyze content to address key business problems such as the following:

- Identify fraudulent claims based on the content of insurance claims forms.

- Measure and monitor customer-service metrics based on an analysis of text in call-center records.

- Plan product-release priorities based on an analysis of warranty records.

- Develop a winning competitive-selling strategy based on an analysis of text in competitor filings and win/loss data.

IBM Cognos Content Analytics is a solution that provides organizations with the tools to unlock the business insight contained in unstructured content.

18

Step 14:
Measure Results

Many Data Governance initiatives have failed because the programs existed to govern data for its own sake. The final step in the IBM Data Governance Unified Process is to measure results against a pre-defined set of KPIs, to ensure that the program continues to drive business value. These results need to be communicated back to the Data Governance council and senior management on a regular basis. Progress against metrics will ensure continued sponsorship and funding of the Data Governance program.

In summary, this book is meant to provide a template for how organizations should implement a Data Governance program. It is meant to remove some of the guesswork out of Data Governance, to make it easier to implement successful programs.

Although Data Governance can never be fully automated, IBM has software tools and best practices to facilitate the overall process, as you have seen throughout this book.

Appendix A

Steps and Sub-Steps Within the IBM Data Governance Unified Process

1. Define the Business Problem

2. Obtain Executive Sponsorship

    2.1 Create a virtual Data Governance working team

    2.2 Obtain support from senior management within IT and the business

    2.3 Identify an owner for Data Governance

3. Conduct the Maturity Assessment

    3.1 Define the organizational scope of the assessment

    3.2 Define the time horizon for the desired future state of Data Governance

    3.3 Define the Data Governance categories to be assessed

    3.4 Identify the right participants from business and IT for the workshop

    3.5 Conduct the Data Governance maturity assessment workshop

    3.6 Socialize the results of the assessment with senior executives

4. Build a Roadmap

    4.1 Summarize the results of the Data Governance maturity assessment

    4.2 List the key people, process, and technology initiatives necessary to bridge the gaps highlighted in the assessment

    4.3 Create a roadmap based on a prioritization of key initiatives

5. Establish the Organizational Blueprint

    5.1 Define the Data Governance charter

    5.2 Define the organizational structure for Data Governance

    5.3 Establish the Data Governance council

    5.4 Establish the Data Governance working group

    5.5 Identify data stewards

    5.6 Conduct regular meetings of the Data Governance council and working group

6. Build a Data Dictionary

    6.1 Select a data domain

    6.2 Assign data stewards to maintain key business terms

    6.3 Identify critical data elements

    6.4 Jumpstart the data dictionary with an existing glossary of terms

    6.5 Populate the data dictionary

    6.6 Link business terms with technical artifacts

    6.7 Support Data Governance auditing, reporting, and logging requirements

    6.8 Integrate the data dictionary with the application environment

7. Understand the Data

7.1 Understand each data source within the scope

    7.1.1 Perform column- and table-level analysis

    7.1.2 Discover legacy schemas by reverse-engineering primary-foreign key relationships

    7.1.3 Identify the location of critical data elements inside each source

    7.1.4 Identify the location of sensitive data inside each source

7.2 Understand cross-source relationships

    7.2.1 Understand how data overlaps across data sources for critical data elements

    7.2.2 Discover the data lineage and complex transformation logic between sources

    7.2.3 Discover data inconsistencies and exceptions

8. Create a Metadata Repository

8.1 Merge business metadata from the data dictionary and technical metadata from the discovery process

8.2 Ensure the appropriate data lineage

8.3 Conduct an impact analysis

8.4 Manage operational metadata

9. Define Metrics

9.1 Understand the overall Key Performance Indicators (KPIs) for the business

9.2 Define business-driven KPIs for Data Governance

9.3 Define technical KPIs for Data Governance

9.4 Establish a dashboard for the Data Governance maturity assessment

10. *Optional Track*: Master Data Governance

10.1 Appoint data stewards

    10.1.1 Appoint the chief data steward

    10.1.2 Determine the configuration of the data stewardship program (e.g., by IT system, organization, or subject area)

    10.1.3 Identify executive sponsors for each data domain

    10.1.4 Recruit data stewards for each data domain

    10.1.5 Empower the Data Governance council to oversee the data stewardship program

10.2 Manage data quality

    10.2.1 Establish data quality policies, including the identification of high-value data attributes

    10.2.2 Baseline data quality

    10.2.3 Build the business case

    10.2.4 Cleanse the data

    10.2.5 Monitor the data quality over time

10.3 Implement Master Data Management

    10.3.1 Identify the business problem

    10.3.2 Define the subject areas of master data

    10.3.3 Identify the systems and business processes that consume the data

    10.3.4 Identify the current data sources

    10.3.5 Define the data attributes of the system of record

    10.3.6 Appoint data stewards for each system of record

    10.3.7 Establish policies for Master Data Governance

    10.3.8 Implement a data stewardship console for manual intervention and monitoring

    10.3.9 Manage potential overlay tasks

    10.3.10 Match duplicate suspects from the same source or from multiple sources to create a new master record

    10.3.11 Link related records from multiple sources

10.3.12 Review duplications of unique identifiers

10.3.13 Manage relationships

10.3.14 Manage hierarchies

10.3.15 Manage groupings

10.3.16 Architect the Master Data Management solution

11. *Optional Track:* **Govern Analytics**

11.1 Define the objectives of the BICC

11.2 Prepare the business case for the BICC

11.3 Determine the organizational structure of the BICC

11.4 Agree on the key functions of the BICC

12. *Optional Track:* **Manage Security and Privacy**

12.1 Align with key stakeholders

12.2 Gather the enterprise security architecture blueprint

12.3 Tighten database change controls

12.4 Automate the compliance workflow process

12.5 Define sensitive data

12.6 Discover sensitive data

12.7 Classify and tag sensitive data

12.8 Encrypt sensitive data

12.9 Protect sensitive data within non-production environments

12.10 Monitor applications for fraud

12.11 Prevent cyber-attacks

12.12 Redact sensitive information within unstructured documents

13. *Optional Track:* **Govern Lifecycle of Information**

13.1 Establish an information architecture

13.2 Baseline database sizes and storage architecture

13.3 Discover business objects

Appendix B

Sample Data Governance Charter (for a Manufacturing Company)

Definition of Data Governance

Data Governance is the orchestration of people, process, technology, and policy within an organization to leverage, optimize, and maximize data as an enterprise asset. Just as our board of directors governs the enterprise to maximize shareholder value, the Data Governance program is intended to maximize the value of data for key IT and business stakeholders.

Business Objectives

The organization has a stable SAP environment, but not all our data is in SAP. It is intended that the scope of Data Governance will increase over time, as the program is able to demonstrate success. However, over the next 12 months, the Data Governance program will focus on supporting the following business objectives:

1. Customer-centricity

2. Vendor management

3. Supply chain optimization

4. Financial data quality

5. Management of the lifecycle of electronic documents and email

Executive Sponsor

The chief information officer will act as the overall executive sponsor of the program, working closely with the lines of business and key functional areas.

Organization

The focal point for the Data Governance program will be the director of data governance.

The Data Governance council will have ultimate oversight responsibility for the program. The council will be chaired by the chief information officer and will include the senior vice president of marketing, the senior vice president of supply chain, the chief financial officer, and the general counsel. The Council will meet on a monthly basis, at least initially. The director of Data Governance will be responsible for setting the agenda of the Data Governance council, in conjunction with the chief information officer and other members.

The Data Governance working group will be chaired by the director of Data Governance. The working group will consist of members from marketing, supply chain, finance, legal, data architecture, and content management. These members will have day-to-day responsibility for dealing with data-related issues within their respective functional areas. The Data Governance working group will meet on a weekly basis, at least initially.

Metrics

The Data Governance working group is responsible for establishing a scorecard of key metrics to monitor the performance of the Data Governance program. The director of Data Governance is responsible for reporting on these metrics, on a regular basis, to the Data Governance council.

Data Stewardship Community

Data stewards have custodial responsibility for data within their domains. The executive sponsors for key data domains are listed below:

- Customer data: senior vice president of marketing
- Vendor and materials data: senior vice president of supply chain
- Financial data: chief financial officer

The executive sponsors will appoint data stewards who will be responsible for data quality on a day-to-day basis. The director of Data Governance will have oversight responsibility to ensure that the data stewardship program is implemented consistently across the organization. The data stewards will be responsible for defining, gathering, and reporting on key metrics relating to their data domains on a monthly basis.

Appendix C

Sample Job Description (for a Data Governance Officer)

Objectives

- Operate as a focal point to treat data as an enterprise asset, similar to any other physical asset.

Business Ownership

- Ensure that the Data Governance program is aligned with key business priorities, such as the customer-centricity initiative sponsored by corporate marketing.

- Improve the quality of customer data to optimize the effectiveness of decisions based on that information.

- Drive data ownership into the business.

Metrics

- Define Key Performance Indicators (KPIs) to monitor and track Data Governance results.

- Report results on a regular basis to the Data Governance council and key executive stakeholders within IT and the business.

Organization

- Drive visibility and awareness of the benefits of the Data Governance program across the organization.

- Set the agenda for regular meetings of the Data Governance council, chair meetings, and manage results.

- Ensure that key IT and business stakeholders stay engaged in the Data Governance program by ensuring that the Data Governance council is focused on the right strategic issues facing the business.

- Oversee the Data Governance working group that meets on a regular basis, and ensure that its activities are consistent with those of the Data Governance council.

- Oversee the data stewards who report into the business. Ensure that data stewards operate consistently, and that the business continues to see value in the program.

Appendix D

Sample Data Governance Maturity Assessment Questionnaire

This appendix provides a sample set of questions to assess the maturity level of a Data Governance program. These questions should be used to rate the program on a scale of 1 (lowest) to 5 (highest).

Here are the guidelines for each maturity level based on the Capability Maturity Model (CMM) developed by the Software Engineering Institute:

- *Maturity Level 1* (initial)—Processes are usually ad hoc, and the environment is not stable. Success reflects the competence of individuals within the organization, rather than the use of proven processes. While organizations at Maturity Level 1 often produce products and services that work, they frequently exceed the budget and schedule of their projects.

- *Maturity Level 2* (managed)—Successes are repeatable, but the processes may not repeat for all the projects in the organization. Basic project management helps track costs and schedules, while process discipline helps ensure that existing practices are retained. When these practices are in place, projects are performed and managed according to their documented plans, yet there is still a risk of exceeding cost and time estimates.

- *Maturity Level 3* (defined)—The organization's set of standard processes is used to establish consistency across the organization. The standards, process descriptions, and procedures for a project are tailored from the organization's set of standard processes to suit a particular project or organizational unit.

- *Maturity Level 4* (quantitatively managed)—Organizations set quantitative quality goals for both process and maintenance. Selected sub-processes significantly contribute to overall process performance and are controlled using statistical and other quantitative techniques.

- *Maturity Level 5* (optimizing)—Quantitative process-improvement objectives for the organization are firmly established and continually revised to reflect changing business objectives and are used as criteria in managing process improvement.

The following is a sample list of questions to be used to assess Data Governance maturity.

1. Data Risk Management and Compliance

- To what extent is the Data Governance program tied to the overall risk management framework of the organization?

- Is risk management a key stakeholder within the Data Governance council?

- Have you conducted an assessment of how the Data Governance program can improve the overall effectiveness of risk management?

- Does the risk management organization agree with this assessment?

- Have you defined a set of metrics to monitor the performance of the Data Governance program, from a risk management perspective?

- Do you have a process to track, analyze, and report against these metrics on a regular basis to the Data Governance council?

2. Value Creation

- ❏ Have you identified the key business stakeholders for the Data Governance program?

- ❏ Have you identified the key business benefits from the Data Governance program?

- ❏ Have you obtained sign-off from the key business stakeholders on the business benefits of Data Governance?

- ❏ Have you developed a business case to support specific Data Governance initiatives?

- ❏ Have you defined key business-driven metrics to monitor the performance of the Data Governance program?

- ❏ Do you have a process to track, analyze, and report against these metrics on a regular basis to the Data Governance council?

3. Organizational Structures and Awareness

- ❏ To what extent do you have senior executive support and sponsorship to treat data as an enterprise asset?

- ❏ To what extent do you have awareness across the organization to treat data as an enterprise asset?

- ❏ Do you have a Data Governance council with strong participation from the business?

- ❏ Do you have a Data Governance working group with strong participation from the business?

- ❏ Do you have a full-time Data Governance officer?

- ❏ Have you established a Data Governance charter, with clearly defined objectives that have been agreed to by senior leadership and the Data Governance council?

4. Policy

Data Governance policies provide high-level direction in how an enterprise will manage its data. Examples of Data Governance policy include the following:

- *Master Data Management at a multi-line insurer*—Policyholder data is owned by the enterprise, not by individual lines of business such as life, P&C, and retirement services (at a multi-line insurer).

- *Data stewardship at a manufacturer*—Data stewards shall focus on customer, product, and vendor data as core subject areas. The data stewards for the customer, product, and vendor areas will report into the sales, research and development, and supply chain groups, respectively. The data stewards will be responsible for ensuring the quality of the data within their respective subject areas.

- *Metadata*—The Data Governance office shall maintain a data dictionary of key business terms. Data stewards shall be responsible for ensuring the correctness of data definitions within their subject areas.

- *Privacy*—The Data Governance office shall maintain a record of all database fields with personally identifiable information (PII). All new database requests to access those fields shall be approved by the chief privacy officer, or her delegate. Privileged users such as DBAs shall not be allowed to have access to PII. This policy also applies to consultants and outsourcers who have database access.

- *Records management*—A records management policy shall be developed by the records management team, covering all types of documents, including paper, electronic, and email. This policy shall determine the master list of document types, set retention schedules for each document type, and agree on the tools to be used to implement the strategy.

Here are the high-level questions to assess the level of Data Governance maturity around policy:

- To what extent is the Data Governance program involved in the setting of policy?

- Are the Data Governance policies documented?

❑ How frequently are the Data Governance policies reviewed and updated by the Data Governance council?

❑ To what extent is the Data Governance program involved in the enforcement of policy?

5. Stewardship

❑ Does the organization have data stewards?

❑ How are the data stewards aligned (by IT system, organization, or subject area)?

❑ Which IT systems are aligned with the data stewardship program (CRM, ERP, financials, others)?

❑ Which business organizations are aligned with the data stewardship program (sales, marketing, finance, risk, others)?

❑ Which subject areas are managed by the stewardship program (customer, broker, vendor, chart of accounts, employee, location, product, materials, others)?

❑ Does each data domain have an executive sponsor who is responsible for the data being "fit for business purpose"?

❑ Are there any plans for enterprise-wide data stewards by subject area?

❑ Do the data stewards own the definition of the attributes of their respective data domain? (For example, is the customer data steward responsible for the definition of the term "customer"?)

❑ Are the data stewards responsible for defining and monitoring key metrics relating to the quality of data within their domains? How often do these metrics get captured?

❑ Does the data stewardship program have visibility and sponsorship across the organization?

❑ Does the business recognize the value of the data stewardship program?

❑ Is there a chief data steward who is responsible for the overall consistency of the data stewardship program across the enterprise?

6. Data Quality Management

- ❑ Does the organization have a standard set of data quality metrics that have been agreed to by the Data Governance council?

- ❑ Have you documented the issues with data quality in your systems?

- ❑ Do you have general agreement between IT and the business about the data quality issues in your systems?

- ❑ Do you have general agreement between IT and the business about the causes of poor data quality?

- ❑ Have you developed a business case for addressing data quality issues?

- ❑ Do you use any data quality tools?

- ❑ How often do you gather the data quality metrics?

- ❑ What is the process to analyze and report on those metrics to the Data Governance council?

- ❑ What is the process to take corrective action on the data quality metrics based on feedback from the Data Governance council?

7. Information Lifecycle Management

- ❑ To what extent have you set policies around the types of paper documents that will be digitized?

- ❑ To what extent have you set policies around the retention and deletion of paper documents, electronic documents, and email?

- ❑ To what extent have you set policies around the archival of electronic information, whether structured or unstructured?

- ❑ Have you established the business case for archival in terms of key value drivers, such as improved system performance and reduced storage costs?

- ❑ To what extent do you have an automated process for eDiscovery?

- ❑ To what extent do you have automated content collection and classification rules that are tuned for adaptive needs?

❑ What percentage of your core business content (for example, lending documents, for a bank) is being leveraged for analytics?

8. Security and Privacy

❑ Does the Data Governance program set policies for security and privacy?

❑ Is the chief information security officer a key sponsor of the Data Governance program?

❑ Is your organization subject to any privacy regulations (such as PCI DSS or HIPAA)?

❑ Have you failed any privacy audits?

❑ Do you encrypt any PII or protected health information (PHI) in your systems?

❑ Do you use unencrypted PII or PHI data within development or test systems?

❑ Do you have database administrators, contractors, and other third parties who have unencrypted access to PII or PHI data?

❑ Do you monitor access to PII and PHI data by users with super-user privileges (such as database administrators)?

9. Data Architecture

❑ Does the Data Governance council set standards for data architecture (such as databases, reporting tools, analytics tools, ETL tools, Master Data Management tools, content management tools, and records management tools)?

❑ Is there a process to enforce compliance with data architecture standards that have been established by the Data Governance council?

❑ Do you have a business case for rationalizing the data architecture?

❑ Have you identified systems of record for specific subject areas, such as customer, vendor, and product?

10. Classification and Metadata

- Do you have a dictionary for key business terms?

- Which subject areas are covered by the data dictionary (such as customer, product, and vendor)?

- Which business organizations are covered by the data dictionary (finance, risk, marketing, sales, other)?

- What percentage of the key business terms by subject area or business organization have been populated within the data dictionary?

- Do you have agreement with key business areas around the terms in the data dictionary?

- Do you have a standard definition for the term "metadata"?

- Do you have a metadata architect?

- Do you have a repository for technical metadata?

- Does your technical metadata repository drive impact analysis? (For example, what is the impact on the data architecture if a row or table is dropped?)

- Does your technical metadata repository support data lineage all the way back to the source systems?

- Are you capturing key operational metadata metrics?

- Have you developed a business case to support technical, business, and operational metadata?

11. Audit Information Logging and Reporting

- To what extent do you have a strategy to reduce the number of out-of-process database modifications?

- To what extent do you have appropriate internal controls to ensure the certification of reports for financial and regulatory purposes?

- To what extent do you have the ability to monitor changes by super-users, such as DBAs?

- To what extent do you have the ability to audit all changes to critical data?

Appendix E

Sample Data Governance Declarations

by Marty Moseley

Marty Moseley is Chief Architect, Healthcare Transformation, IBM Information Agenda, and former Chief Technology Officer of Initiate Systems, Inc.

Declarations are the primary deliverables of a Data Governance initiative. They are based on a shared vision and reach often-difficult agreement between all affected parties (usually the business leaders serving on the Data Governance council). They enable the business to tailor its actions to meet discrete business goals and objectives, which are always paramount in Data Governance. They also give specific directions and guidance to those who are responsible for operating the business. Some declarations are written by data stewards, some are written by business analysts, and some are written by architects. All declarations that address the cross-functional sharing and management of data should be approved, or ratified, by the Data Governance council.

For declarations to be effective, they should be "SMART":

- Make a specific Statement of "who," "what," "when," "where," "how," and "why"

- Are Measurable and auditable

- Can be Acted upon

- Are Realistic and relevant to business objectives

- Are Tangible—not abstract, theoretical, fuzzy, or vague

The declarations of the Data Governance initiative fall into a number of categories: principles, policies, procedures, business rules, and metrics.

Principles

Principles are the highest-level declarations of why the quality of certain classes of data matter to an organization. They address the value of the class of data to the organization, or the value of achieving certain levels of quality for the data. They may address the mission of the organization, the behavioral mores expected, and who benefits from the end result; as such, they are almost like mission statements or statements of purpose for companies. Principles will usually declare the breadth of reach, scope, and detail of the oversight, by answering the following questions:

- Why is this Data Governance initiative being undertaken?

- What are the business needs, risks, objectives, costs, and opportunities that underlie this initiative?

- Why do the following policies and actions need to be undertaken and executed?

Principles are written, approved, and ratified by the Data Governance council. They reflect the value and importance of data at the highest organizational levels, not "down-in-the-weeds" operational viewpoints.

Here are examples of principles:

* Establish the overarching criticality of data.

Overarching Data Management Principles: Quality, Safety, and Perfection

The quality of critical data— patient and physician data being the most obvious—are paramount to the effective healthcare outcomes and the continued success of <organization>. The safety of our patients and staff will be protected at every stage of admittance, diagnosis, treatment, and follow-up. Ongoing practices will be implemented to ensure the ever-increasing levels of quality that are required by <organization>. Changes to requisite jobs will be made to ensure an appropriate investment in skills training, to ensure that patients' data is protected, and that <organization> retains the best staff available.

With very slight wording changes, the same could be said of customers' data for commercial organizations or citizens' data for government organizations.

* Address the necessity of a Data Governance council.

Breadth of Oversight and Representation of <organization>

Critical to the success of the Data Governance council is the unbiased, balanced, cross-organizational representation of <organization's> goals and objectives. Every attempt will be made to ensure that goals, objectives, risks, issues, opportunities, and priorities will be balanced across <organization>. Data Governance council members will represent their specific organizations, but always with a view toward the most critical priorities for <organization> as a whole.

* Address the criticality of a master data domain.

Principle for Patient Data

High-quality patient data is absolutely essential to achieving the mission, goals, and objectives of <organization>. In this way, patient data is considered a highly shared enterprise asset. Every effort shall be made to ensure that the data we capture and manage on behalf of

> *patients is of the highest quality, is available at every point of care, and is protected for the benefit of our patients and <organization>.*

Again, with very few wording changes, the same could be said of customers' data for commercial organizations or citizens' data for public-sector organizations.

Policies

Declarations of policy make measureable statements of what must be achieved to realize the goals of a principle. A policy does not state how it is to be achieved; that is specified by procedure and business-rule declarations. Policies can refer to internal or external standards, regulations, rules, or guidelines (such as privacy guidelines) and can require compliance with legislation such as SOX and HIPAA. Policies make the following statements within a principle:

- What are the levels of quality that must be achieved for each type of data?
- Who owns the responsibility?
- How are exceptions and disputes handled?

Policies may be written by data stewards, members of the Data Governance council, or members of various adjunct boards, panels, committees, working groups, project teams, and so on. They require significant negotiation to ensure that the scope and detail are right.

Here are examples of different types of data policies:

- Definition policies
  - *"A citizen is an individual party who has (past, present, and future) a direct or indirect (inherited) citizenship relationship with a country."*
- Content, structure/schema, and semantic policies
  - *"Each constituent record, if it is an organization, must have a valid business address and a valid shipping address, plus at least one company has contact relationship with an individual."*
  - *"Each consumer record must, at minimum, have an enterprise identifier, at least one consumer name, a billing address, a telephone number, and an email address."*

- ❑ *"Postal address must conform to standard XYZ."*
- Integration policies
  - ❑ *"Each system exchanging citizen data must translate its local schema into the INDIV.XML schema v3.5.1.2a."*
- Security policies
  - ❑ *"Property Bill of Materials is treated with a confidential security level."*
- Ownership and remediation policies
  - ❑ *"Land management owns all decisions regarding structure and content of location and all subordinate entities."*

Procedures

Procedures, also referred to as "processes" and "practices," are declarations of how a policy's goals are to be achieved. They define the tasks that, when executed, achieve the mandates (objectives or requirements) of a policy. Declarations of procedures define how, when, and where policies are enforced, and by whom.

Here are some topics that are addressed by procedures:

- Who does what, and when they must do it
- Who is involved, and in what capacity (whether they are merely informed, consulted, or the approving body)
- The proper sequence of steps to perform certain actions
- How exceptions are handled
- How actions are communicated

Business Rules

Business rules are discrete specifications of how a piece of data will be evaluated to see whether it meets a policy's quality goals. They provide detail into how to treat specific data anomalies within a policy, and they describe the following:

- Which data elements are critical

- Which values and relationships are valid (or invalid)

- How to determine whether a value is correct or allowable

- What to do when a value falls outside the bounds of what is considered acceptable

Business rules can call upon reference data to check for allowable values, or they can call a profiling engine to check on the validity of a set of data. They are usually written by data stewards, programmer/analysts, and business analysts. They are very detailed, and far below the purview of the executives who make up a Data Governance council.

The following are examples of business rules that might be written during a Master Data Management engagement:

- Uniqueness rules: *"An <entity> is uniquely identified by... within a specific context."*

- Domain integrity rules: *"This field has only <these> allowable <values/ranges/formats/masks>."*

- Semantic rules: Meaning, accuracy, consistency, validity, usefulness.

- Currency rules: *"This data is good only until <date-time stamp>."*

- Usage rules: Who has requested this data.

- Referential integrity rules: Must include keys of referenced data; dependent data must be properly created before/after.

- Security rules: Who is allowed to see/use which records and fields for what purposes; who may share data with whom.

- Structural rules: *"The object must conform to <schema definition>," "users will get the <fields> back in this order. . . ."*

- Set rules: How many records can be used at once.

- Volume constraints: *"Users can get only <n> records at once."*

- Performance constraints: *"Users will get data back in <nnnn> seconds."*

etrics

vered in the body of this book, metrics are declarations of what should be
asured to ensure the successful achievement of a set of business objectives.
ey are the critical data elements captured about transformations that provide
ight into the quality of a piece of data. Metrics are also meant to measure
progress being made toward achieving business goals stated by policy
clarations (in support of principles).